James J. G. Wilkinson

Revelation, Mythology, Correspondences

James J. G. Wilkinson

Revelation, Mythology, Correspondences

ISBN/EAN: 9783337242152

Printed in Europe, USA, Canada, Australia, Japan

Cover: Foto ©Andreas Hilbeck / pixelio.de

More available books at **www.hansebooks.com**

REVELATION

MYTHOLOGY

CORRESPONDENCES

BY

JAMES JOHN GARTH WILKINSON

JAMES SPEIRS

36 BLOOMSBURY STREET, LONDON

1887

CONTENTS.

—— 0 ——

CONTENTS.

The Unknown and the Unknowable : The Savage Men of the
Study, ... 108
Egypt, ... 115
Compound Animal Forms in the Word and in Mythology,   . 124
The Age of Myths is past,   .   .   . 129
A Mode of Origin of Myths, ... 129
The Origin of Correspondences in the Adamic Men, .   . 131
Adam and Eve, the Proprium, ... 132
Inspiration by and Revelation from Jehovah God began all
true Manhood, ... 134
Declensions Perpetual, ... 136
Restorations Perpetual by and from the Divine : Successive
Churches, ... 138
Heathen Religions at the Side : their Ways and Means,   . 140
Uses of Mythologies as Schoolmasters and Art-Masters in
Language and Æsthetics, ... 144
Primeval Perception and its Streams of Memory and Tradi-
tion, ... 146
The Remainders of the Heathenisms   .   .   . 149
Ethnologic-Geographical Light will come of the Biblical
Revelation of the Churches, ... 151
Attestations from the Word. Nebuchadnezzar's Dream of the
Image. Daniel's Vision of the Divine Restorer,   . 154
Divine History and Human History,   .   . 156
There is no such Thing as Pre-historic Man, and no such Man
as the Fontanellian Savage,   .   .   . 157
Man's Epoch, and when he was put into Natural Creation,   . 161

APPENDIX.

PREFACE.

THE DOGMA OF PROGRESS.

1. THEOLOGY has suffered perversion from the dogma of *Juventus Mundi* conceived as implying progress as a necessary part of the career of the social and individual man. He cannot stand still : he is constituted in movement ; but whether this shall be for good or for evil, for better or for worse, depends upon himself, and upon no necessity outside him. It has depended in all ages upon his reception, either in his heart, or in his conscience, of the religious guidance that was offered to him. Therefore at no period of the world's history has the general

A

mankind been launched from infancy with the fate of becoming adult in intelligence, and wise in the end. This happy, and by no means fated, result has been secured by individuals in all ages, through religious faithfulness, whatever the religion, provided it contained in any measure an acknowledgment of a divine Being, and command of a life according thereto. But only by a false analogy can this be applied to the race. The race has not grown up from infancy, through a virtuous youth, and steadfast middle age, to a good old age. There is no progress of that kind for man : none but a contingent and dependent progress. On the contrary, the Fall has been written out in Sacred History, and attested by profane history, many times ; it is strongly attested to-day ; and the inference is that man of himself is a creature of the Fall ; and that if he and his societies have not fallen utterly, and perished from their place, some Lord of life apart from man is the Redeemer and Sustainer.

2. One demonstration of this is afforded by Progress itself: by Progress or forward rapid movement which is considerable in this age and cannot be ignored. There is a dark spirit accompanying the progress; a spirit of pride and self-adoration which is hostile to the spiritual and moral elements and conditions on which truth leading to good depends. It is a subversive spirit, and leads to a fall, and a progress in falling. Now indeed it can only lead to individual and national decadence; but that is terrible enough. The Redeemer and Saviour has the future in His hands, and His Church is secure. But the creed that the race is necessarily rising to more excellent life by its own progress is at war, in the votaries of this creed, with whatever can be done for them from above.

3. There is no adult infancy of the world
but a divinely communicated and humanly
received Innocence and the Wisdom of it;
no Adolescence but the same indwellings
growing and confirmed; no full Age but
the same virtues again confirmed in constant
humility and love: and there is no decay,
decrepitude, or dying out, but selfishness,
corruption, and sin.   As at first, so now, progress worth the name is everywhere subject
to these conditions.

4. Without careful heed to them, it is not
possible for Churches, States, or individuals,
to be aware if the speed which urges them
is towards human good, or backwards from
it.   They cannot know otherwise whether
they are in the broad, or the narrow way,
on the road to life, or destruction.   An
illustration may suffice.   The weapons of
modern warfare, — there is incomparable
progress here; but is it forwards for the

Christian man, or backwards? Science, Art, Wealth; all the self-born virtues, and their emulations; hatred, revenge, and glory, second murderous skill and invention; and tread the winepress of battle. But does not the very existence of particular societies and nations depend upon these violent arbitraments; and does not the wealth and permanence of the faculties of violence also likewise so depend? Is not that vague general boast, civilization, at the mercy of the violence; to say nothing of the substance of common freedom in homes? And are not the issues in the hands of the most unscrupulous and evil men, exalted by excess of self-love into demoniacs?

5. This is from the gross temporal side; and dominion over souls and minds from the invisible spiritual side, is even more destructive. It destroys the man internally; and at the same time con-

dones and indulges the outer works of his
devil.

6. The moral is, that all speculations
about the human race, and the lastingness
of particular parts of it, are futile, which do
not take account of the regeneration of
individual men, in which alone the new adult
infancy, adolescence and manhood can be
achieved and found. Civilization, whatever
it mean, and Savagery, are alike destitute of
these epochs. They can come but slowly.
Each evil thing in an individual has to be cast
out, and stopped from becoming hereditary.
The proportion of men and women in which
this arrest is effected, determines the ad-
vancement of the race; the Lord being
constantly acknowledged as the Giver of its
victories and the Father of its good.

7. There is then no continuous development of mankind *per se*, but only fatal
evolution of consequences; spiritual gravi-

tation in person, space, and time. The
Laureate says truly "that through the ages
one increasing purpose runs," but more
doubtfully, that "the thoughts of men are
widened by the circle of the suns." The
increasing purpose is of God's mind, not of
man's; but the widening of the thoughts
otherwise by solar procedure is temporal,
geographical and mechanical; and in nowise just or integral. Thoughts were
widened so in Egypt, and so in Assyria;
but the width did not last; it had not the
broadness of the " truth of good."

8. Progress as an idol has vast human
sacrifices to answer for : whole races offered
up to it in immolation. This is one
reason of our iterated refutation of the
current dogma of the savage man as the
well-head of life and history. We have no
quarrel with the savage, but only difference
with his mistaken patrons. Livingstone on

his last visit to England said of his dear
Africa which he was looking forward to,
" My many friends are there ; all of them are
heathens, and most of them are savages."
This is intelligible and humane; and the
savage is in a good almoner's care.   But he
is out of place as a speculative beginning of
religion and church, and also of mythology.
He is no tent of the most ancient worship ;
no floor to the Tabernacle of Abraham; and
no foundation stone, ever so minerally
subterranean, to the Temple of Jerusalem ;
still less to the New Temple. He fits
into no such edifices.   Neither theoretically
into societies as edifices.   And to pose him
as having " a field-marshal's baton in his
knapsack," is to make progress fatal and
venomous.   It means that he has his
cunning demagogues ; and rises up through
their creed, by his own right, into the mind
of rule as an admitted factor.   Godless

progress, of which he is the assumed
beginning, implies this. It means no divine
guidance, and therefore is the permitted push
of all the lusts of "the natural man." Take
two Statesmen, one of them a volume of
programme and progress, who obeys and
hothouses the likings and tendencies of his
masses; the false hopes and ideals: and
another, who holds their deluge at bay; and
letting whatever can endure, endure as long
as ever it rightfully can; altering wisely
without hearkening to dictates from below:
and you will have two results to justify our
positions. First, that Progress as an idol
and a heathenism immolates the races it
pretends to serve. And second, that Progress when it means Wisdom in wide action,
is the curb and blessing of mankind, and
the unflattering conscience and religion: the
progress of self-control. Also the place of
issue of stable liberty and its strong militia.

9. Observe that the idolatrous progress
now so largely represented, pleads Fate, and
is actually the *ultima ratio* of the savage
man, and of his modern representative, 'the
people, the only source of all legitimate
power.' The other progress, of which little
may be extant, is founded in Freewill, and
knows by its special intellect that ages
may elapse before any of its ideals can be
gratified; and also that the best and highest
ideals can never be realized here below.
The difference between the progress from
the savage upwards, and from the wise man
downwards is illustrated in every human
mind which attends to conduct. In regard
to attainment of professed objects, it is the
difference between the impossible and the
possible. The confirmed minions of fate
are bound to its abysses; to the final com-
pulsions and the " eternal workhouses." The
men of Freewill, leaning upon its trials and

ever correctible reasons, have two boundless futures before them, — *indigenæ utriusque mundi;* and a promised Kingdom.

10. The reader, it is hoped,—the gentle reader,—will excuse, and even appreciate, this preliminary walk, before entering a wide field of dissertation, into some practical consequences. No belief is so abstract, especially if it comes from the inward places of the will and understanding, as not to beat, with the force of its descent, or the gush of its ascent, with its free inspiration, or despotic invasion, upon the ultimate platform of deeds and works; at first in a single mind, and then in larger and greater fields of power. And this is the justification we offer of our disproof and rejection of what at first sight may seem a harmless creed,—the dogma of progress from the savage man.

PRELIMINARIES.

THE OCCASION OF THIS ESSAY.

11. THE present slight attempt to indicate an origin and place for Mythology not generally accorded to it, was immediately occasioned by *Fontanelle's forgotten common sense*, an article in THE ST. JAMES'S GAZETTE, of Oct. 20, 1886. The writer's solution was the scientist view, that whatever is odd and strange in Mythology, whatever is hieroglyphic in distinction to plain modern type; whatever is not in literal accord with the experience and exactitude of the present day; and cannot be tested as strict sensual fact by evidence and especially by science;

is to be relegated *ultimately* to the untutored
strivings and upward gropings of the savage
man.   He is to be reckoned the original
Poet of it.   And he is judged heavily by
the learned essayist, almost as if he were an
author deserving criticism, for his presump-
tuous mistakes and ignorance of the latest
agnosticism.   I have attempted to show that
he is not guilty of the alleged authorship, and
that far other names and races are entitled
in it, and endorse it.

EVOLUTION *VERSUS* CREATION.

12. The attitude of the scientist, I will not
say, scientific, and of a part of the literary,
I must not say, learned, world, to this
department, Mythology, is maintained in
the current teaching of the materialist
schools with respect to nature generally
and her origins and issues.   Evolution is
the name for it.   While holding absolutely

that for mankind, and for all species of
things outside, rising from the ranks is the
order, discipline, and law, we hold besides
that there is a divine marshal who is the
source of this militant merit - order, and
Who has revealed Himself as such. His
therefore is the promotion from the dust
to the man, from the man to the angel, and
from the present to the future. Regarding
this merely as a theory, it would be hard
for the learned Essayist to say, after the
chain of evidence I produce, that the latter
view does not run through the facts, and
is not as workable as the contrary position
of the world - outcome from the savage
man. It might even seem that the writer
whom I thus meet is on the other hand guilty
of Myth, and in this particular is in the ranks
of those he looks down upon. And if so,
then a great part of our modern thoughts
about nature and her inherent tendency and

progress, is myth in an uninspired sense;
namely in the risible sense in which our
friend means all myth: in the sense of
guesswork and strong baseless persuasions.

THE SAVAGE MAN PROPER AND THE SAVAGE MAN UNIVERSAL.

13. The savage man is becoming extinct
in two ways. In the first place, regarding
him as the *savage proper*, there is less and
less room for him in the spaces of the
human world. His generations stop,
stricken by their *uselessness.* The foothold
of man in creation is USE. The savage is
of less and less use to the brethren, to the
general humanity. Contact with other and
higher races, even interbreeding, which
might be supposed to improve the species
in him, destroys him. It is for him a fatal
mesalliance, a mixture of destructions. He
cannot withstand the vicious mind and body

of civilization, the drinks and the lusts; they require a stronger constitution of wickedness than his poor timber, to outbreed and outlive them. For he is naturally, with no help for it, near his end.

14. In the second place, there is another savage man, also with an origin from degeneracy, but with a different scope in him, and, maybe in some rare cases, with a different future. In distinction to the savage proper, we may call this one the *savage universal.* He lives in the human woods and wildernesses, in the deserts of man: really, though not always visibly, beneath the bottom of the social scale. The savage proper is in no relation to the social scale, pressed upon from above by no inequalities, but absolutely free for ruin. But the other savage is ground down, and might it would at first seem also be ground up, and like plaster of Paris, harden towards

a new social individual,—if he chose. Who is he? By him we intend the mass of helpless and decaying people, who, with bodily powers intact or with powers ruined ancestrally or personally, are of no use to our *Maximus Homo*, to orderly organic society. These savages are the *opprobria* of civilization; the disgrace of the state. They exist in all ranks and classes, from noble to simple; but in multitude at the lowest end. A constant product of all ages, they are especially numerous in luxurious times. They are circumpressed by society. If you could weed them out in mass from the body corporate, and plant them away from civilized intercourse in sufficient tracts of wood and wilderness and hunting-ground, the survivors of the exodus in a generation or two would be all equal socially whatever their ancestry; they would forget the previous towns and conditions, and would realize liberty and fraternity as such words could belong to them. They would be forced to foray for hourly subsistence. They would be found clothed with the skins of brutes if they were visited, and would descend through the bronze and iron ages to the stone age; and would improvise the lost arts in "celts" and flint implements.

Parallelism between the two Men.

15. Thus much requires to be said to justify the view that the savage man is a necessary decay and *detritus* wherever mankind is on the downward slope, with religion dying out, with conscience devoid of a divine inspirer and ruler, and with moral life at the mercy of the selfhood or *proprium*, of the abundant lusts and pretexts of which it becomes the voluntary institute and creation. Accordingly, in seeking for this justificatory universal savage, we find

him in the useless man in all ranks and conditions. We do not here intend the criminal classes, the active artisans and workmen of hell; nor the sick and impotent, who deserve all help, and loving pity; but the loafing man who is in some relation and respect to society, though not of it. All those, in fine, who whether well or ill have no "good of use" in them. As we said above, this savage man is imprisoned in society. In fact, he disappears in it, and is content so to disappear; his denomination is not known, and one has need of a philosophical pin to pick him out like a whelk from his shell of clothes. Indeed one reason of his invisibility is, that society puts compulsory cloth, more or less complete, or ragged, upon him. Also there are no waste spaces for him to escape to, and stand out. He comes now into a full world, whereas the savage proper went down into a deserted

and emptied world. He is gendered for
the most part in cities and towns, and
submits to their necessities because he
cannot get out of them. What regeneration awaits him we know not. If not
actively evil, he might be educable, and
emerge from *ne'er-do-weel* and loafing, and
leave charity undiseased by parasites on its
head and in its heart. But otherwise, like
the savage proper, he dies out; though his
remains are concealed by civilization; and
in that respect have not the same interest
for the scientists as the bones and implements and kitchen-middens of the savage
proper. Of course he originates nothing
but his own breed, and this for a time.
And as you get no mythology from the
savage proper, so you get no art or common
sense, no Shakespeare, Bacon or Tennyson
from the *civilizee* savage. We note then
that there is a running parallelism between

the two savages, of cause, mode, and con-
summation; only taking into account the
different circumstances between the more
primitive world, and the world of primogeni-
ture, and of broad acres, deserted country-
sides and villages and big towns, of to-day.

Consequences of putting the Savage Man in his Place.

16. It is pleasant to be candid, as our great
Bismarck is. And therefore we avow one
object, and that a principal object, of these
and the following humble studies. We have
long seen that if the savage man can
be truly and justly displaced from the
throne which he now occupies in the
imagination of the heart of scientism, and
stand no longer as the virtual seed and
blood royal of humanity, his overthrow will
have good consequences of riddance, and a
world of inferior wild pretenders will clear

out along with him. The series of *infima*
of which he is the last and most important
link, will be confronted in him, and denied
their "pass;" and will no longer extend
fungoid relations to man; unless in the
confession of admitted parasites, external
or internal; so to be caught and dealt with.
This, while denying no progressive order,
will admit from above and from within,
creation which scientism abhors, and be
a safe frontier of wise fortresses against
the insurgent demos of things. The frontier
is of ends and causes, with substantial
garrisons of uses, and is held by One
Divine Man in Whom they love and live.

17. Divine intervention, unremitting and
continual, is thus the fact and the law
of every successive rank, and one rank
never passes into another. No mineral
can become a vegetable; no vegetable can
ever be an animal; and no animal a man.

A great gulf, spiritual, is fixed between each plane, and between the upper and lower corresponding creations of each. Ordained *form* is the castle of each individual creature in all its multitudes, and that castle is impregnable. And according to the form is the creative influx into it. And therefore it is that the forms of life live; that the forms of vegetation grow; and that the mineral form in all its varieties underbuilds and materiates the rest. The man-form is a man with a conscience on the same conditions; but of spiritual form and organism. All descends from above, or what is the same thing, comes forth from within.

A PLEA FOR THE SAVAGE DISALLOWED; HIS CASE DOES NOT BEAR IT.

18. There is a possible consideration in which scientism might still entrench and

defend its savage man, and put him forward as the *fons et scaturigo* of all our good things. This namely. That the primitive savage is not lightly to be identified with the perishing savage tribes as we now know them, in Tasmania, Australia, and elsewhere. The vernal age of the savage should not be confounded with his winter. For the beginning of every true race has a zest and a spring in it which is lost to power and freshness as the series oldens. Young love's dream illustrates here. Might Fontanelle's presumed poetism of the savage be an instance of this? The assumption of such a fellow begs the question. For this new savage would be an abstraction without a Genesis to lean upon, and no relation to the old bones which are all we know of the real savage man; who by his ways and means is clearly on the same level in arts and senses with the existing tribes of savages. I do not suppose that the above plea would be acceptable to scientism, amounting as it does to the claim that the early wild man was an infant of delights, a man of joyful genius, and was himself a golden age. But were it taken up, it would be a piece of the true doctrine, which is, that man was created as a special human form with no ancestral evil heredity, though on the lowest scale of faculties and powers, and was raised by his creator and maker through a process of divine education to his first estate when he became a Celestial Man.

19. But otherwise the presumed origin of the presumed primal savage is not a ground for regarding him as a promising young man, the launch of " the argosy of the ages." The current view of his museum-keepers is, that he is the child of the Lucretian slime-world, and hails from a

low form of mollusks. Genius is joy, and wants joy to live in. All birth too, after its throes, comes into a prepared world of mother and father, and the first smiles and laughs of infants light and warm the world. But the evoluted man comes by no love and no parturition, but is made by the struggle of his motherless self before he is a self. How for the delight that begins all good things is he different from the slime and the fish, his wombless misfortunes ? We must therefore give him up as the babe of grace and the first poet ; and be content with the old ultimate savage as scientific sextons turn him up, and then turn him over and over.

REVERSION TO THE ORIGINAL STOCK BESETS AND THREATENS HIS HONOURS.

20. Great promise is held out on the other hand by the eminent Sir John

Lubbock in the very nudity and pocket-
lessness of the savage man as compared
with the elegant wealth of his presumed
children,—Art, Science, civilization, the moral
and the social worlds, natural religion, and
above all, endless progress and advancing
light and liberty. These, the alleged works
and institutions of his scientist descendants,
are indeed *longissimo cœlo* apart and away
from the bogmen and the cavemen, and
the flint implements. If the push and
generative impetus of the wild men have
kneaded up so vast a result, they are indeed
both promising and performing savages.
It is admitted by Sir John that a few
great slips have occurred in which empires
have tumbled out of men's hands, and
broken to pieces. Nay, not a few. The
earth is raised and thickly covered with
their potsherds; and the ruin is directly
traceable to the baseness and evil of men.

But still the sum and substance of this
present age, for instance, is large and
surprising if credited to the troglodytes.
And yet the breakages of the self-made
crockery are a ground of fear for the
whole promise of the savage man, and for
the ratiocinations spun from him. And for
a reason of science. Is there not much
Darwinian true talk of reversion to original
types so soon as culture is intermitted
or careless. Chrysanthemums ungardened
are poor little flowers soon, and roses the
same. Men also can easily become lower
than brutes, and nations of such men cease
to be nations.

21. Reversion to the original type is
therefore on the evolutive ground a perilous
prospect; indeed an abyssal perspective.
For the first sad landing downwards is
the savage man himself, with all the train
of cities and civilizations, religions and

societies, progresses, and scientisms, "tele-
scoped" and wrecked back in him by the
first collision with fate. But he cannot
stop here; or rather he does stop here;
and his ancestry, the headless mollusk, and
the pregnant mud, in cruel series, inherit
further backwards in the advancing degra-
dation-field : and in the end the mineral
and gaseous and fire universes, the presumed evolvers of his extinguished life,
are the bottomless executors and adminis-
trators. The consolation is that these are
worked up again somewhere else into
similar ignominies. And so on for ever
and ever through "the boundless realm
of unending change," which is built of the
two biggest tumours in the pondering ovaries
of materialism, infinite time and infinite
space. Sure, the mud had better have been
downright humble mud, and the fish have
kept to his just scales. This, which is here

set down is, however, the plain end of all
boastings about and hopes from the savage
man as an aboriginal.   It is the blue
empyrean of our admired and in his own
walk our admirable Tyndall.

22. On the other hand, the Divine Man
showing Himself by Revelation, and giving
Human Religion perpetually forth to acknowledgment and life, is the true account of
all the manhood we possess, and of all
the natural blessings we enjoy; and the
denial of this Lord, and the heresies of
ourselves, are the sound explanation of all
our savagery, and of all our natural curses.

MAN IN THIS WORLD IS AN INEVITABLE
RELIGION AND SUPERNATURE OF SOME SORT.

23. Man has been called a religious
animal, and the phrase has a truth in it.
The original impress of Jehovah God upon
him is so almighty, that even if he becomes

an animal, that dictate never leaves him, but resides as a remainder in his nature, and lives as religious tendency through all his surviving vicissitudes. From this ground the entire substance of humanity down to a late period, has never, in any sane part of it, been nature alone, but has always been charged more or less feebly with supernature. So much is this the case that the naked apprehension of sensual facts has been a late invention and dis- covery, and is difficult to be maintained by the scientific mind without a continual controversy on the road with religious influxions. Even so great a scientist as Proctor keeps up a running fight with these throughout his spirited bagpipe-march from matter against spirit. All poetry, all painting, has been thus impressed and influenced; and absolute realism is still afar off, realism enlisting all the mental

faculties. The reason is that there is a
God Who reveals Himself and hides Himself; and where He hides Himself, Atheism
is compelled to grope after Him in many
ways, and to invent towards Him in many.
Pressure from above, tradition from behind,
necessity of decency around, all work this
way. And there is only one Worker. In
this age, however, natural fact in its mere
omni-mental veracity, craves to be sought
and told; and the reason here is that
spiritual fact, to which as ultimate truth
it belongs, wants it, as pyramids want
their bases, as society wants honesty, and
as Heaven wants its seedfield, the Earth.
And the final reason is that since the
Incarnation, and the perfect doctrine of it
now vouchsafed, the Christian Religion is
not only a Divine but also a strictly natural
and rational Religion; and therefore finds its
testimony in all truth, and will repose upon it.

REVELATION AND
MYTHOLOGY.

REVELATION TOUCHING CORRESPONDENCES.

24. "At this day it is not known what CORRESPONDENCE is : but in the Most Ancient times it was of all things well known.   To those indeed who lived then, the Science of Correspondences was the science of sciences ; and it was so universal that all their Tablets and Books were written by Correspondences. . . . I am instructed that the men of the Most Ancient Church, which existed before the Flood, were of so celestial a genius that they spake with the angels of heaven, and they were empowered to speak with them by and through corre-

c

spondences.   Hence the state of their
wisdom came to be such in regard to
whatever thing they saw in the world, that
they thought of it not only naturally, but
spiritually at the same time; therefore also
conjointly with the angels of heaven.
Furthermore I am instructed that the
Enoch who is spoken of in Genesis v. 21–24,
and those who were with him, collected
correspondences from the lips of the most
ancient men, and propagated the knowledge
of these correspondences to posterity.   In
consequence of this, the science of corrre-
spondences was not only known in many
kingdoms of Asia, but also was cultivated
and worked, particularly in the land of
Canaan; in Egypt, Assyria, Chaldea, Syria,
Arabia; and in Tyre, Sidon and Nineveh;
and from thence it was carried over into
Greece; where, however, it was turned into
Fable, as may appear from the oldest

writings of the Greeks." Swedenborg, *True
Christian Religion*, n. 201, 202.

MYTHOLOGY.

25. The absurdities of mythology is an
easy theme to a scientific and anti-
mythological age; say in a word, to an age
of ratiocination and so-called rationalism.
It is forgotten that the greater part of what
we know of classical mythology is handed
down to us in poetry, and was presumably
not what it appears to be, an everyday
creed of religion influencing the minds of
the common people. There is no reason
to think that mythology stood in any such
relation to the mental condition of any
race, savage, or civilized, as, for instance,
dogmatic Christianity to-day occupies to the
hopes and fears of the nations which profess
it. Parts of mythology were indeed known

to the heathen conscience, as containing
the general belief in a future state; the
whole true doctrine of the Elysian Fields,
and of the retributions of Tartarus, are
among these parts; but Jupiter and Juno
and the Gods are aside of them. So also
for the warlike North. Valhalla is a
general record of an immortal state less dim
and more gross than the Elysian Fields;
but there is nothing to show that the
commonalty of the Northern Races was
influenced in its everyday mind and
consciousness by Odin, Thor and Tyr.
These personifications, however they originated, dwelt in heroic poetry, and became
a part of it, and appealed to the popular
mind from this embodiment.

26. A separation is here discernible
between a residual religion which had
still some guidance in it, and a mythology
which now belonged to the imagination,

the fancy, and the senses; and which has to be accounted for.

27. A corresponding separation may be found for the same races between mythology as a lever of causation, and their plain appreciation of causes and reasons in everyday life. Like ourselves, and in some departments more than ourselves, they were artisans and handicraftsmen, workers in metal, potters, architects and artists; also farmers and manufacturers, cultivators, breeders of stock, hunters, and militant tribes and peoples, beautiful in bow, sword, spear and shield. The notions of causation now attributed to them were no factors in their day's works. In the mass of the people such notions were hardly extant. The myths supposed to hold them would soon have died out had they not been conserved in Poetry and Saga. As there was no natural philosophy to speak of in the days

coeval with the birth of mythology, so whenever curiosity about origins arose, the folks perhaps shrugged their shoulders in poetry and saga, and ended questions, not vexed by them as we are. But they did not think as we think that they had solved them. Their lives were natural and practical notwithstanding the presence of mythology in their midst. The great works and traditions, the penetrating influences, these races as wholes have left behind them, are in evidence here.

28. Also they had kept for them somehow, perhaps by their poetry in some union with their common sense and natural religion, a vital characteristic in both departments, the religious and the philosophical,—that when they did attempt to enter either, they were not skeptics, or deniers of everything that lies beyond the senses. This kept the supernatural open for them in a measure;

it rendered them willing recipients of the gifts of all their Muses ; and made them fontal in the style and manner and institution of the great Literature which by Providence has followed in their wake.

29. In limiting the actual power of mythology over the classic world, of which we now chiefly speak, we cannot forget that besides the mythologies we have also the temples of the Gods and Goddesses still standing over the South and the East, and corresponding heathen edifices in the New World, and in ruder lineaments in the Scandinavian North. These signs betoken something which we must call worship all over the world in those extended days. But was it anything of what we now mean by worship? Was it ecclesiasticism or meeting, was it church or chapel? Was it even anything like the worship of the Virgin and the Saints in the Romish Church?

The question is an interesting one, and touches upon the whole possible *piety* in our sense of the Greek and Roman times. If it was not worship, what was it ? Rather it seems to have been an institution of festivals of self-indulgence in the name of the Gods ; voluptuous festivals, whether of sensualism, or asceticism ; festivals of which we have a faint survival in the social doings of Christmas and Easter in Christian lands. For given the phenomena of Christmas and Easter, and the problem being to account for them in the main,—Bacchus and the Satyrs and Pan as presidents might be the resultant induction for many houses. We of course have worship and Christian benefactions besides. The classic peoples also had orgies and mysteries, summaries and paroxysms of sensualism in the guise of religious rites ; an abundant ritualism in this fashion. But their Gods, though personated through matchless sculpture, and enshrined in Doric and Corinthian architecture, had no piety proper attached to them, but were the sanctions of great holidays, and their oracles were sought for assurance and destiny-mongering by their votaries, who, be sure, were not of the common herd. In the manipulation of all this, apart from worship, there was ample room for the existence and maintainance of a powerful Priesthood, as in the Papal manipulation at the present day. And yet it was not worship in the classic period, but the occasional uncontrolled riot of the natural man with pretexts for Gods; and it had no ordaining influence over life. The corollary is, that this mythology with its shrines, oracles and temples, however it might lend itself to their lusts and vices, yet by no means befooled the people in their common human faculties in the manner supposed by those who assume that the myths are the evolution and creation of the savage man himself, and that in them he is bound in his own chains. On the contrary, we begin to suspect, that they are not the product of the savage; and were so to speak palmed upon civilized populations, descending by methods not difficult with knowledge now to hand, to comprehend; and did not greatly injure their intelligence for the reasons already stated. For if at one time almost everybody received the mythical Gods, no one in a rational sense believed them: and common reason was thus intact.

IDOLATRY.

30. This leads to the question of *Idolatry* with the same races. We commend the subject to the learned as a new field. A chasm exists between the Eastern Empires

with Egypt, and Greece and Rome in this
respect.   The Worship of Baal in particular,
with its great Priesthood, was a genuine
Idolatry; and human sacrifices, even of sons
and daughters, entered into it.   The Gods
of the nations required propitiation in this
way.   These rites flourished among the
grandest communities in Biblical times.
They were altered traditions of the representative sacrifices of the Ancient Church,
and survived in Christianity in the sacrifice
of the Son to appease the wrath of the
Father, and in the atonement supposed to be
effected thereby.   This indeed attributes
the mind of fallen man to God, and deprives
Him of His unity.   But it also attests the
earliest knowledge by perceptive revelation
that Christ would be a sacrifice in a true
sense as the Redeemer.   A proof that these
powerful idolatries were the perversions of
a high primitive estate.   The Gods of the

nations which the Israelites were commanded to war with and exterminate, were the objects of this idolatrous Worship.

31. In Greece and Rome the case was different, and the idols were of a milder kind. It is doubtful whether human sacrifices were perpetuated there. As Swedenborg says, the ancient correspondences which were at the root of all, "in Greece were turned into Fable." The personalities of the Asiatic demonolatry there disappeared, and the Grecian Gods were human Greeks on a higher platform. Note the progress here. It was a progress not from any savage state upwards, but came after huge heathen civilizations and priesthoods; and after the Israelitish and Jewish Churches had been planted by Jehovah in the world. It was a permitted degradation and diminution of colossal idolatries, in which idolatry itself in its combat with Christianity

at length in its nominal forms died out; to survive however and stream onwards in the Romish Babylon. The Grecian deities descended from a new spiritual world into a natural world already charged with the coming of the Saviour; mythology in them was shorn of its greater infernalities, and a chastened humanity such as the Greek could represent was portrayed in some of his Gods.

SUPERSTITION.

32. It occurs to remark that idolatry and mythology occupy in some sense an inverse relation to superstition. Of course they are penetrated and permeated by it. But their forms absorb it, and it exists as a sphere around them, rather than as a Figure. The more definite the idol and the more developed the mythology, the less do the panic fears and reasonless hopes of man prey upon the universal inane. They are

concentrated upon the Gods so far as any
religiosity exists. Pan himself becomes one
of the deities, and is measurably limited
thereby. The dynasty of his fellow
divinities compels a human shape upon
him. The condition of a superstition thus
absorbed is not found to any extent unless
as a dying remainder among savage tribes.
Accordingly, except for their fetishes, which,
however, have no particular individualities,
they live in a limbo of vague superstition.
The remainders of all the previous churches
and races like disembodied ghosts are about
them, but in no recognizable shapes, and
the "cosmic sense" of these ghosts is the
very element of superstition. Savages may
indeed at times, through extraordinary
persons and occasional magical influences,
escape back in part into their lost mythological condition ; but otherwise they have
no mythologies, only fear of their own

dead men and women. And they stand not as the beginnings but as the plain ends of heathen humanity; itself the termination and mortification of a series of churches.

33. The same thing holds in a higher sense with Christians. The Lord is their Shepherd. The Divine Humanity of Christ is their personal Redeemer and Saviour. In proportion as they hold to this, their daily lives and cares are taken up, borne, and absorbed by Him. In proportion as they quit the Divine Image, they live in the superstitions of their own minds; in the carving out of their own destinies beyond the day; in fears for the future; and in fortune - tellings about death through the stars, the cards, and " the spirits."

34. The superstitious state may be put aside or abjured, it may be cast off by instruction received from without, but it can never of itself be developed into a higher

condition.   There is no radical element in it
but the lapsing savage man, the soil of decay.

35. There is an image of all things in
all things.   In London to-day there is a
lowered image of the world since the
beginning.   There is an upper, lower, and
middle stratum of spirits and bodies with
their several intentions, conscious and un-
conscious.   The lower is not developed
into the higher, though the higher may
degrade itself into the lower, and the lower
by a godly life may raise itself and rise into
the higher.   But the classes as wholes stand
in their own lines though individuals circulate
up and down in them.   The savage men at the
bottom, of whom there are many, are not the
parents of the future age, and do not portend
or attain to its spiritual or bodily culture.

FONTANELLE'S FORGOTTEN COMMON SENSE.

36. Coming now to Fontanelle as reported

by the learned Essayist in the *St. James's Gazette,* we observe that his great man believes that "the early men were in a state of almost inconceivable savagery and ignorance," and that the Greek and other myths are inherited from human beings in that condition. That the first narratives of the earliest men were full of monstrous things "because they were given out by people bound to see a great many things which had no existence." This, says Fontanelle, was helped by such "philosophy" as was even then extant, and which made men look for "causes of things." (A philosophy which, on this view, raised itself through a line of Greek thinkers from Thales to Aristotle and Plato.) And as these poor savages experienced that they were themselves causes of effects, as well as persons, they "sprang to the con- clusion that all hidden causes were also persons." In which case their minds were facile to universal and general propositions; and capable of striking near the centre.

The Greek Mythology originated in Greece ; piecemeal, but rapidly.

37. Now with regard to the position that the Greek myths were inherited from a race "in almost inconceivable savagery and ignorance," what is the ground on which it stands ? Where is the Greek mythology, full of narratives, genealogies and details now summarized in great dictionaries, before and out of historic Greece ? Where is the record of the bare savages from whom the Greeks were descended ? All we can know of the place of their mythology is, that it probably originated *as we have it* in Greece. And as Minerva came full-armed from the aching brain of Jove, — what a divinity-symbol is there, — so the masterpieces of

Greek mythology came fully formed from— What ? We shall hope to find a dawning answer to this in the sequel. In the meantime we assert provisionally that man is a spirit among spirits at his best and at his worst, and thus always in the background has exceptional powers which beasts have not ; powers more or less. There is a history of Greek Literature, but no similar history of Greek Mythology. Part by part it probably originated oracle-wise in cursive hours when the race was charged with it, and ripe for its birth. *Völuspá* originated thus in the North in its fulness of time ; a Vala, an entranced Seeress, spoke it forth. It was taken into record and memory, and ages repeated it. It did not require a longer labour than Sir Isaac Newton wanted for receiving the concept of gravitation ; though his was a somewhat different kind of *passivity*. Such births, if we knew the mode

of them, never take long in their several
pieces.   In the case of mythology especially
they are mere concepts; they involve no
cudgelling of the brain, and can be worked
out no further.   They want no alteration.
They are given in full armour, such as it is,
whether of gold, or of brass.   Fontanelle
knew nothing of this kind of birth, and
accordingly thought that this mythology,
which no doubt came from different tripods
bit by bit, but always in short *seances,* was
the product of the fogs of a struggling
causative faculty, and developed itself in the
Darwinian method through prehistoric ages.
But reason as we see had nothing directly
to do with it; and when once the mythological oracle-door was opened, the multitudinous details would come forth in one or
two generations.   Not but what it could
proceed from grosser to finer, like all human
inventions, whether of Poetry, Drama, or any

kind of art and invention : but this is not development from savagery or the brute degree of the genus *homo*, but starting from an adequate and powerful germ, and then following the inevitable course of all human powers and seeds in the succession of time : the womb of some aiding form of society receiving and nourishing them. The new advance may indeed be a plane of fall from a previous state ; but it transacts its own stages, and makes a traject through them, having a rise, a culmination, and a decline.

38. History is full of these lessons, and in all great or typical nations there are such series observable. In our own country we have the age of cathedrals, the age of drama, the age of railways, the age (now) of railway novels. When these realizations have done their work, ages of other genius prevail. Each series is produced by its own spirits, muses, or causes. The age of mythology

came so, but it could come on only Delphic
conditions.

EACH MYTHOLOGY ORIGINATES FROM AND WITH ITS OWN TRACTS OF HEATHENS.

39. As the Grecian Mythology as an
organic product originated in Greece, so also
every Mythology arose in its specific form
in the countries in which it had place and
power, and in a sense was the product of
the land. Thus the Indian Mythology is
essentially Indian, and is of, and like, the
Indian peoples. The like is true of the
Scandinavian Mythology, the specific attributes of which belong to the northern
peoples, and are peculiar to them, extend-
ing where they extended and penetrated.
There is no known case of the transplanting
of a mythology to heterogeneous races;
there are no missionary "conversions" of this
kind. The Greek Mythology did indeed

overspread Rome, for the two states were conterminous, and their civilizations were level with each other, and Rome exhibits early traces of being a participator in the Grecian myths. Mythology thus is essentially gentile or heathen. The spirit which engendered it is, however, in each case common to the whole world, and lies in the necessity to the mind of man to acknowledge and make acquaintance with a power above itself, and to open a way, by giving it a Name or names, to that power. The pressure of this necessity on a new race came no doubt as an ancestral spirit from a previous mythology, and was full of its ancient germs; but this spirit, thus seminal, found its soil and matrix in the genius and affections of the new people over whom it brooded, and in them produced a new heathendom and its proper myths. We may say as a rule that down to Christ every

mythology was age by age becoming
smaller, less illustrious in its contents, and
spiritually less commanding and comprehensive. See above, n. 31. The Gods of Asia
and Egypt are awful presences compared to
the genteel divinities of Greece. This dis-
accords with the Fontanellian origin of the
myths from savages upwards; for it shows
that, in association with gigantic architecture,
they have been greatest in the greatest
nations and civilizations; and have under-
gone continual paring down and decline
through one civilized heathenism after
another.

IT COMES FROM MAN, AND IS VARIOUSLY
ANTHROPOID.

40. Fontanelle does not indeed formulate
that the mythologies had a long incubation,
but the factors he assumes lead to this view.
If mythology is a gross and multiform

philosophy of causation, any such product takes time to make, and has to be thought out, and to receive its nomenclature. In this case ages might elapse, and generations of unskilled savages be engaged. But how could their raw material, liable to get into disgust and be forgotten daily, commend itself to memory and tradition? How should Hesiods and Homers treasure it up? These difficulties are removed by the fact that civilized, artistic and poetic races, with divination, magic, trance, mediumship, exciting festivals and mysteries with tripod-sitters in their midst, were the composite field and agency of origin. The Greek mythology also, as already observed in speaking of superstition, was a rescue from materialist pantheism. Truly the Sun wheeling round the world, or revolving in any way, wanted a driver, and Phœbus Apollo, a human god of light, supplied the

want. This was better than material law
excluding divinity : better for the simple
Greek if such there were, than the savage
degree of mere eyesight and sensation
and mathematics. The whole movement
of heaven and earth exacts of the mind a
divine Charioteer ; and the doctrine now,
the oldest and the newest, is, that a personal
God is the mover, a divine Apollo; and
that his appearing residence in heaven is
in a Sun, a Spiritual Sun. And Phœbus
more readily than materialist law, itself a
diffused superstition, is translateable into
this revealed truth.

A Note from the Elder Edda.

41. The Scandinavian Mythology is
strongly *anthropoid* in its own gross way;
and even the stuff of its world is organic,
of Giant-human origin. Thus Ýmir was
a Giant who " lived in the hoar of ages,

when there was neither sand, nor sea, nor cold waves; when the earth was nowhere, and high heaven nowhere; there was the gape of emptiness; but no green herb." Then Mundane things were made out of Ýmir. "Out of his flesh the earth was shapen; out of his bones the mountains: heaven out of the head of the frosty Jötun; and the seas out of his sweat." There is "a method in this madness;" a pointing at the human ground of creation; which is as it were not a raw material, but a prepared pre-organism for the Genesis work of the world-maker. "Let us make Man in our Image;" the mere ground - nature being already prospectively descended from him and full of him. Note also *hrimkaldr Jötun* = frost-giant; as in a certain stage of creation pointing to an era of cold, a purpose of "mighty winters," stopping off the heat of divine ends and intentions, and making the possible temperature which *homo protoplastus* could endure. There is suggestion of wisdom too in the cold head of heaven. In fact this myth like many others is as a seed which can grow into various perceptions.

THE EARLIEST MEN AND THE EARLY MEN:
WHO THEY WERE.

42. Fontanelle speaks as if he knows all about the "earliest men" and the "early men," who however are two very different classes of devolutions. In truth he knows nothing of either of these departed humanities. Bound in the ratiocinations of France, he sees many things which have no existence. One of these *non-exstantia* is, that the earliest men were left to their own unaided state to rise in the human scale. And the obverse, which has existence, and which he does not see, is, that their direct Father, Jehovah God, helped them. The Bible in Genesis,

chapters i. to xi., as Bacon remarks, is
the *only* record there is of the earliest and
the early men; there is no other; it is a
spiritual record of their minds and souls,
which in their variations are the summits
and summaries of all history.

THE CHURCH NAMED MAN OR ADAM IN GENESIS.

43. The Bible tells that the earliest men,
the Church or Inspiration named Adam, was
right in perceiving that "all hidden causes
are personal," because that race was created
and made in the image and likeness of God,
and God is One Person. Those men issuing
from Him, and by direct pressure of His
grace knowing and acknowledging Him,
yea, perceiving Him as their only Life,
could not be pantheists, any more than
a good son loving a good father and mother
could believe that the neighbourhood and

house he was born in had begot him. It
was, however, a late race, and an age-long
degradation of the race named Adam or
Man;—a race that had descended by many
steps;—which, still refusing Pantheism,
coined the fragments of perception, and of
tradition without perception, into personal
myths, of Jupiter and Juno, of Thor and
Odin, of Baal and Ashtaroth, of Brahma
and Vishnu; and which after coining them,
preserved these myths in poem and story,—
in Fable,—and made the mythic persons do
duty *vice* God in not the explanation, but
the artful envelopment of the mysteries of
nature. Even so these myths, "incredible
and revolting" to scientism to-day, conserved
some shaping of the real creative cause in
the personality which lay in them; they
were allowed for late nations and peoples
that wanted them; and their committal to
Poetry was also an accommodation to a

memory that in deteriorating races would have forgotten them apart from the amber-conserving hardness of song. The same poetic form also enabled them to resist the dissolving agency of philosophy when it came upon the scene, and also of any science that might exist, and which of course was averse to gods and goddesses.

PLANES OF PERSONAL CAUSES RECENTLY REVEALED. THE WORLD-TREE.

44. These, the last poetical remainders of the "science of correspondences," have a basis from the spiritual world, which we now know by a knowledge which is experimental and unassailable, to contain all the persons who have ever died from this and other planets. All these are personal causes, and the laws of nature and human nature carry out their causation. They live in "the chance and

change of the unsteady planets." The myths
contain hints and summaries of their presence.
The Edda, with its Yggdrasil, the World-
Tree, the Horse of Odin, the tremble and
vibration of nature — *Yggr* = vibration—
with the many destructive animals that gnaw
and consume its roots, its branches, and its
summit,—that myth is still something for
spiritual philosophy to dwell upon. No man
believed in the tree as a literal tree, any more
than in the trees of knowledge of good and
evil, and of life, in Genesis; but it corresponded, and ever corresponds, to spiritual
experience in the world of men, and to much
physical fact in the world of nature ; and it
has Biblical sanctions and rebukes in it.
And from this example, whatever might
otherwise be said of these Myths, we see that
they are blunt and unsentimental, and do not
foster that modern softening of the brain and
hardening of the heart which is implied in

the Leibnitzian dogma, that "we live in the best of all possible worlds."

Saturnia Regna. Grecian and Scandinavian Mythology attests a Primeval Golden Age.

45. Moreover all the great mythologies contained one core which is especially 'incredible and revolting" to the materialism of the day, which assumes the dregs of the winepress as the source of the wine of the future. They all uttered some declaration of a Golden Age from which the existing man is a decline; and some of them even contained a prophecy of a restoration to come at the end after purification by fire in the fulness of time. Such is the case in Völuspá, the book of creation and generation in the *Edda*. In its close, when slain Baldur, the white, the pure, returns from Hela, the lower earth, to the Earth of men,

E

the nations of the Righteous are received into everlasting happiness by the Ruler come to his kingdom, and the children of the serpent are carried by Nidhöggr, the down-hewer, the destroyer, the "serpent from beneath," to the land of corpses, may we say of the spiritually dead.

46. Again it is prophesied in the Book of the Vala, that after the destruction of the world, which is told in Apocalyptic symbols,— the sun becoming black, and the serene stars falling from heaven,—after the high heat has played against heaven itself,—"the earth rises vernal green a second time from the Ocean ; and the gods meet on Ida-plains; and dis-course of the world-engirdling serpent;[1]

---

[1] In the Midgard serpent which girdles the world we have here another testimony to the Biblical Correspondence of the Serpent in the Word, as meaning everywhere the sensual mind,—*sensuale*,— which is the outermost, or encompassing mind, in which the *amour propre* or *proprium* resides. In like manner with this, nearly the whole of the particulars in *Völuspá* are susceptible of a Biblical interpretation.

and call to mind the powers of fate, and the ancient runes of thrice great Odin." And moreover this. "The wonderful golden tables shall there again be found in the grass; those which they had in the hoar of the ages." What are these wonderful golden tables but the record of the heavenly perceptions written in the hearts of the first men, and now found in Swedenborg's grass, for the understandings of the present men to feed on ?[1]

47. Again it is said in the Lay of Vafthrudnir, that "after the mighty fivefold winter a remnant of man is left; that Life and Life-desire are hoarded away in the wood (holti) on the Mount of Mimir, the golden treasurer," that a people may issue from them in the end of days. "They are fed on the dews of the morning, therefrom are the ages born." Are these things spiritually

[1] "Gramen significat id verum Ecclesiæ quod apud hominem primum nascitur." Thus the restoration of the knowledge of correspondences is in the first rejuvenescence of the celestial Church.

looked at, "gross and irrational," the results of a "state of almost inconceivable savagery and ignorance," or of "mere ignorance and superstition"? Mythology contains others as pregnant. If present Christian belief had died and vanished, and if no Second Coming of Christianity had been vouchsafed, would not such myths better serve the souls and minds of the world's nations and peoples, than Comteism, Darwinism, agnosticism and materialism considered as substitutes for religious creed?

SCIENTISM OPPOSES.

48. Fontanelle and his learned reproducer in the *St. James's Gazette* have indeed not done justice to the Mythologies. Some of their details are absurd, and some light and satirical, though these might be spared pedantic criticism, for they are mostly harmless. But scientism which aims at sensual exactitude feels its dignity injured by their

existence, and cannot let any Myths be. Like a great and admirable scientist who could not bear the words " magic lantern," but would have the thing called *scientific lantern*, lest magic, which was out of his 39 articles, should be mentioned, and advertised.

49. Nor has Fontanelle any glimmer of a rational origin for mythologies. His treatment of Myths, and of the *earliest* and the *early* men, exposes him to the judgment of Solomon : these children are not in his genesis. He is willing to destroy them, and keep the dead halves for anthropological science, but he cannot love them or take them to his breast.

LITERATURE AND POETRY LOVE MYTHOLOGY.

50. Yet surely they must be worth something to the learned, and Literature would mourn them if they were exiled. Take Prometheus out of Æschylus and out of

Shelley, and furthermore as an influence and seed out of the atmosphere of thought and speculation; take Minerva and the rest of the supernatures out of the Odyssey; dispossess the Fates as the spinners of destiny, and Pandora with her box of hope, "sole boon of man;" and a vast amount of pith and beauty, to give these things no higher value, would be cancelled out of humane expression. Scientism will have to settle these values in this field with the Poets. We must leave that bargaining, and come to other considerations.

PROMETHEUS.

51. The learned Essayist asks, "Why we have ceased to tell such tales?" The ages have them, and more are not required. There was once a direct mind-market for the growth; there is none now. That is one reason. Also, the representation of

spiritual things by natural symbols in this manner has ceased as an active production. It descended from the primitive revelation to the earliest men, and took different forms as it passed on in different nations. It became idolatrous. But even here it embraced two factors : 1, Historical Influx, —the traditional atmosphere of correspondences and representations, now an external but still powerful atmosphere of impression ; and 2, an Influx from the spiritual world close above those ages, and pressing into them ; and impregnating them with fragmentary conceptions of the broken divine unity ; producing fables of as many deities as outward nature and human nature suggested to the sensual mind. Still these deities, gods and demigods, were often in the line of the ancient correspondences, and carried a felicitous meaning in their record. The fire that Prometheus stole from heaven

was the self-love with its powerful intellect
and genius severing itself from the divine
love, and originating a line of human inde-
pendencies with which Jupiter was offended;
and the human counsel which arose, looking
before and after, was chained to hard limits,
and had a terrible vision of the state which
it had engendered : given in the eagle which
preyed upon the vitals of this new and
necessarily remorseful but unrepenting *Proprium.* That can be one interpretation.
The fable may have any number of such;
for by necessity of its kind, its possible
contents are fertile like the spawn of fish,
and can fill the ocean of man's thought with
shoals of true suggestions in faculty after
faculty and realm after realm. In that
respect these discredited Fables stand alone,
above all genius and imagination.[1] This

[1] See the author's work, HUMAN SCIENCE AND DIVINE REVE-
LATION, the chapter on *Inspiration and Genius.*

one is an attestation of the Fall of man from a seemingly dependent, but really free, to a seemingly independent but really enchained estate. The high mountain too to which Prometheus was chained in the Caucasus is at once the falsity and truth of the state ; the falsity for Prometheus, the truth for the nature of things. He mightily observes himself and his nature, and the truth observes him.

HERCULES.

52. The labours of Hercules are another myth which might be unfolded through endless discourses : they might be sermons. The eminent Swede, Siljeström, an exceptional Educationist and Scientist, has lately given us one exposition of this Fable, interpreting it well of human enlightenment and Religion, and the purified Civilization proceeding from them. On the subject of Greek Symbolism generally, Rektor

Siljeström says, "The Greek Fables are thoroughly symbolical, and the Wisdom that speaks from this mythology is so deep and so comprehensive, that it is impossible not to see the actual civilization of thousands of years mirrored in it. How many Civilizations have flourished and passed away before man has capacitated himself to perceive the essence of culture as it is given in the Saga of Hercules?" *Tankebilder ur en gammal mans Dagbok*, Stockholm, 1885. Bacon in his *Wisdom of the Ancients*, has shown his sympathy in these things by many fine interpretations, and especially by his remarkable reading of the Myths of the god Pan, which we commend to attention. These and other reverent expositors of the classic hieroglyphs, are considerable counterweights to the virtual "stuff and nonsense" solution of Fontanelle and his learned successor.

SWEDENBORG'S READINGS. CORRESPONDENCES :
THE HORSE.

53. Swedenborg, while marking these
things in contrast with Revelation, and even
with Assyrian, Asian and Egyptian mythologies, by the diminutive distinction of
Fable, yet has given indications for the
interpretation of certain of them ; thus
attesting that some hand of the most
ancient divine cypher is upon them, and
that they can and will be considered with
profit by spiritual men.   An example of this
occurs in his reading of the Winged Horse
Pegasus, a blow from whose hoof caused
the fountain of the Muses, Hippocrene, to
spring from Mount Helicon.   Bellerophon
mounted this horse, and with his aid
destroyed Chimæra.   Bellerophon was the
son of Sisyphus, the doomed hero of the

rolling stone in the place of punishment.[1]
The horse, biblically, signifies the understanding; a winged horse, spiritual-intel-
lectual understanding.   The apocalyptic
horses that came out of the Book, the
Word, the white, black, red, and pale horses,
signify the present understanding and
estimation of men as regards the Word;
for what other thing comes out of a book
when read than the understanding and
estimate of it?   The White Horse on which
the Son of man rode is the power of
the pure truth of it.   The armies in
Heaven followed Him on White Horses,
that is, lived in pure unfalsified understandings and life-followings of Him, the

---

[1] The horse is sometimes used in this sense in common discourse.
When Emerson lectured at Nottingham, Joseph Neuberg, the
translator of Carlyle's *Frederick*, asked him to explain something he had said in a discourse, which request Emerson evaded,
" For I am not riding that horse now." A correspondential way
of saying that he was not then in the spirit of that understanding
of things.

Logos. And wherever the horse is mentioned in the Holy Word, it signifies either true, or false, understanding. This is now, since Swedenborg, a universal induction valid in all particular instances. It challenges disproof. Pegasus has the signification of some spiritual understanding; the blow of his hoof is the ultimate sensual power of it, unlocking on *Mount* Helicon— mountains are Love, states of goodness, "how beautiful on the mountains are the feet of those who preach glad tidings"— the fountain of the Muses, Hippocrēnē, the Horse-fountain; the understandings and sciences of all the muses, which are the ultimate effects and lives of all daily inspirations of goodness upon earth. Bellerophon on this understanding is also the destroyer of Chimæra; he dissipates the fogs and hesitations that confound Use and action.

54. Swedenborg's words are (in translation) : " By the Winged Horse, Pegasus, the Ancients understood the intellect of the truth by which wisdom is attained. By the hoofs of his feet, the experiences through which natural intelligence comes. And by the Nine Virgins, knowledges and sciences of every kind. These things are now called Fables, but they were correspondences, from which the primeval people spoke." *True Christian Religion*, n. 693.

55. Mythology, therefore, in its better parts, is parallel in its interior sense with the Scriptures of the Old and New Testaments.

PROOFS OF THE TRADITION OF THE MOST ANCIENT CORRESPONDENCES AMONG THE ASIATIC NATIONS.

56. Swedenborg reckoned also with the existence of correspondences among the

Asiatic nations, in which however the correspondences did not so much take the shape of mythical Fables, as of direct tradition altered and heathenized, and often converted into magical powers and usages. The correspondences used in some instances were however real and "most ancient." The Greek Fables were unlike this *in powers;* they were a new point of departure in a lesser race more distant from Man or Adam; and they had no ultimate magic in them; but were æsthetic oracles, more or less significant. The following shows Swedenborg's sounding-line at work in touching on correspondences among the Asiatic nations.

57. " To make it evident that the science of correspondences was long preserved among the nations in Asia, that is to say, with those who were called diviners and wise men, and sometimes magi, I will

adduce the following instance from 1 Sam.
chaps. v. and vi.   We are there told that the
Ark, containing the two tables on which
the ten commandments were written, was
taken by the Philistines, and placed in the
house of Dagon in Ashdod, and that Dagon
fell upon his face to the earth before it;
and a second time that his head and both
the palms of his hands lay broken from
his body on the threshold.   Also, on
account of the Ark, the people of Ashdod
and Ekron, to the number of several
thousands, were smitten with emerods,
and the land was devastated by mice.
The Philistines, therefore, summoned the
priests and diviners, who, to stay the
deadly destruction, came to this counsel.
They were to make five golden emerods
and five golden mice; and a new cart;
and to set the Ark upon it, with the
golden emerods and mice beside the Ark,

and to have the cart drawn by two milch
kine tied to it, and bellowing[1] in the way
before it. The Ark was then to be sent
back to the children of Israel, by whom
the kine and the cart would be offered up
in sacrifice. And thus the God of Israel
was appeased. It is plain from the
signification of these several measures
prescribed by the Philistine diviners, that
they were correspondences. The signification is as follows : The Philistines themselves
signified those who are in faith separated

---

[1] The kine were to be separated from their calves. The
text says, "bring their calves home from them : " *i.e.*, break
their natural affection for their offspring. The authorized version
also has, "lowing as they went," but bellowing is what happens
under the circumstances. It indicates the strong compulsion that
was on them, evidently supernatural, to "take the straight way"
in opposition to their natural love : according to Swedenborg's
interpretation. Here it may further be observed, that the Philistine diviners were acquainted with the history of the Lord's doings
for the Children of Israel and the Egyptians in Egypt ; for they
said to the Philistines : " Wherefore then do ye harden your hearts,
as the Egyptians and Pharaoh hardened their hearts ? When he
had wrought wonderfully among them, did they not let the people
go, and they departed ? "

F

from charity. Dagon represented that
religious state. The emerods, with which
they were smitten, signified the natural
loves, which are unclean if separated from
spiritual love. The mice signified the
devastation of the Church by falsifications
of truth. The new cart signified the natural
doctrine of the Church, for in the Word
a chariot signifies doctrine from spiritual
truths. The milch kine signified good
natural affections. The golden emerods
signified the natural loves purified and
made good. The golden mice signified
the vastation of the Church removed by
means of good; for gold in the Word
signifies good. The bellowing of the kine
in the way signified the difficult conversion
of the concupiscences of evil in the natural
man into good affections. The sacrifices of the
kine with the cart as a whole burnt offering
signified that in this manner the God of

Israel was propitiated.   All these things
which the Philistines did by the advice of
their diviners were correspondences; from
which it is plain that the science of
correspondences was long maintained and
kept up among the Gentile nations."
Swedenborg, *The True Christian Religion,*
n. 203.

Similarity of Myths all over the World—New Zealand.

58. Fontanelle observes that mythical
remainders are similar to themselves all
over the world; which he attributes to
the fatal absurdity of the primitive savages
following everywhere the same natural
lines of development.   We remark however that the races which produced the
myths are nowhere extant.   Their geographical scope demonstrates, as Bacon

clearly saw, a radiation from an original dynamic centre.

59. Such remainders exist among the New Zealanders, said by some to be now the finest of the savage races. Sir George Grey has a book on their fables. One of these represents that Heaven and Earth were at first close together, and touched each other, so that there was no room between them. But trees arose—trees— and pushed up the heaven or sky; and held earth and heaven apart. Note that in Genesis trees also in the most ancient men parted earth and heaven. Trees are perceptions more or less, in this case lessening and lowering perceptions. These early men preserved as history by this myth, wanted room for the play of their own wills and ways, and it was accorded to them in the perception that they had it not, in which case they were permitted

to take it. They felt the primeval nearness of heaven an intolerable pressure on their lusts, and they had a new and to their perception independent property of self given them whereby they could live in their own *state-space*. A pregnant record that the Creator from the beginning has allowed mankind to develop of their free-will one plane of humanity after another, each different from, and lower than, that preceding it; the history of all the early part of these various and successive human natures being kept for coming generations, for great purposes, in the casket of myths. Through Scripture and through mythology, the history of created man is written imperishably; his whole arcane mind is displayed; and Revelation furnishes also the divine complement which could not fail; showing by historical correspondences how the Lord has followed the permitted outgoings of His creature, and provided successive means for his upholding on each stair of the descent; and for his final restoration.

THE ISRAELITES OUTLIE FONTANELLE'S VIEWS. WHY?

60. The learned Essayist says further : " Making an exception for the Israelites, Fontanelle concludes that all nations made the astounding part of their myths while they were savages, and retained them from custom and religious conservatism." But why this exception which disproves the rule ? If the Jews were not savages, and if the Old Testament is in the category of myths, and if Scripture is an indefeasible power in the world, is there not here, in visible generation, an origin of myths which contravenes the position taken by our respected Author, that myths arose in the vague and vacuous dark-

ness of savagery; for here we have them breaking forth in the midst of a great, pertinacious and everyway peculiar people. Also they came compulsorily and rebukingly to that people, who constantly disregarded them, and in spite of the thunders of " Moses and the prophets," could not abide the prescription of *their* " Myths," but disregarded the teaching, and fell continually out of the lines of " religious conservatism." Moreover they knew nothing of the correspondences in which the prophetic Word was written ; a manifest sign that the spirit of the age, the Jewish *Zeitgeist,* had nothing to do with the production of the Prophecies, except to give them the comminatory form which made them applicable to the froward indomitable Jews.

AND THE CHRISTIAN CHURCH AT ITS BEGINNING.

61. And why an exception for the Israelites

and not for the Christians at their beginning ? According to Fontanelle's drift, much of the Gospels must come under the head of Myths, and the whole of the Apocalypse. And yet these visible origins eighteen hundred years ago, shed no light of confirmation on the dictum that myths are the product of bare savages. Here of course we assume with the sceptics that the supernatural in Holy Scripture, wherever it occurs, is myth. But in this case it is no struggle after causes and reasons, no making of philosophical dolls in savage nurseries, but viewed in all the con- sequences that have come of it and been connected with it, it is a portent that has nothing to do with philosophy in its dawn, but with philosophy at its wits' end; the portent of salvation, or damnation ; of heaven, or hell.

Myths are the Natural Future States of Precedent Lost Revelations.

62. Myths then properly so called are the consequence of the decline and dying out of Revelation and its commandments, and are not the beginning of philosophies. The mapping out of the astronomical heavens into signs, the Bear and the Virgin, Orion and the Pleiades, are indeed, besides convenience for knowledge and nomenclature, mythical strivings to connect the things of the natural heaven with the things on earth; in which respect they are again derivations from the ancient and inextinguishable Science of Correspondences. But the races which originated these things were highly scientific races, much addicted as in Egypt to the Science of Religion such as they had it; and on the

merely human scale the long opposite of savage tribes.[1]

THE UNIVERSAL COMPASS OF EXACTING AND CONSEQUENTLY EXACT SCIENCES.

63. For there are sciences of all things. We have sensual, physical and mathematical sciences, and it is supposed that these are the only clear sciences. But all real Biblical fact and correspondency is also a subject of science when it is ascertained. It is the mightiest and most imperative of sciences. So is all that belongs truly to the Church of the Lord. So all the dealing of man with man ; all human law, justice and judgment, is a science. It can all be taught, in order that the good and true way may be walked in. And from the cognitions or knowledges of these

[1] Sir Charles Lyell, speaking of Egypt with the writer, averred that the myths of death and judgment and futurity, in that land, were an anticipation of the Christian scheme, and that they travelled over the lines of Bunyan's *Pilgrim's Progress.*

many and many sciences, depend in time all true intuitions even in the sensual, physical, and mathematical spheres. That is to say, they depend for their persistent will and permanence on the religious sanity of man. It is a matter of influx into different faculties. And therefore science, the legitimate child of conscience, has been possessed in its kind and measure by all races ; but has no beginning, but a vanishing end, among the savages. These therefore have initiated neither sciences, philosophies, nor myths ; nor the germs of them ; though they may be devastated by the worms of the final superstitions of all the three faculties.

A UNIVERSAL SERPENT-MYTH GIRDLES THE WORLD.

64. The influx of that earliest correspondence-record of the Fall of Mankind by the instrumentality of the serpent, has been of

such power, pressure and prevalence, that the tokens of it are extant in myths inherited by whole races, and in the fragments of extensive edifices in Great Britain and France; and even now in Serpent-worship in Africa and the West Indies.   The Vaudoux rites involving cannibalism, and the serpent which is their centre, and which is sometimes installed if not enshrined in the Catholic Churches, have been described by Sir Spenser St. John, as he knew the circumstances in Hayti.[1] Vaudoux is an importation of the black magic of the Negro races in Africa.   A sign also that those enduring races are not savages in the sense of decadence; for they maintain their myths, as they also increase and multiply.   This test may be applied to other races; and account for the state of the North American Indians, who seem to have fallen

---

[1] *Hayti, or the Black Republic :* London, Smith, Elder & Co., 1884. Vaudoux is called *Vodun* on the African coast.

in Historical times from builders of Temples to the position of hunters which they now occupy. They have their Great Spirit, and happy hunting fields beyond the Grave, yet they are dying out, and their myths are dying with them, though Longfellow is their Hesiod and Homer.

65. The serpent - myth is perhaps the most remarkable traditive survival of the race called Adam, of which the primeval church emphatically named Man in Genesis was formed. The details of the serpent-worship into which this divine correspondence was degraded are gathered up in a learned Treatise, " The Worship of the Serpent traced throughout the World, attesting the temptation and fall of Man by the instrumentality of a Serpent-Tempter ; " by the Rev. John Bathurst Deane, 1833. This book may be especially recommended to New Church readers who wish to pursue

the present case in its connexion with the correspondences in Genesis. It shows that even the names of places in our own country are derived from man's ubiquitous serpent. There are two ends to the story. The first is that the inspired Genesis transcribed from the ancient archives, and brought by Moses to the Jews, gives an origin for it which is given nowhere else, and adopts it into the Religion which dominates the conscience of the world. The second is that the races which have degraded it into Myth, *dracon-tium* and serpent rites, are not the origin of it, but receive it without comprehension, now indeed by "custom, and religious conservatism." In this fashion serpent-myths are perpetuated in India, and the Emperor of China sits on a dragon-throne.

THE GIANTS OF REVELATION AND OF MYTHOLOGY.

66. Genesis i.—xi. is the source from which the mythical giants of the heathenisms are derived. As before remarked, this part of the Word is not historical, but quasi-historical, written in Correspondences suitably to the genius of the men of the Most Ancient Church. Adam and Eve are primeval Man created and made in the image and likeness of Jehovah God, in whom self-love and its dark persuasions of the mind had not yet risen into rule. This Man was no bigger in his own esteem than his Maker designed him to be. He was the child of God, and innocence made him so, and innocence is small to itself, and great only to its Maker. When this Adam declined in posterity, and ceased to be,

men had grown mighty in self-assertion,
and their proprium ruled over the primeval
religion. This in a measure is not difficult
to comprehend. Every wicked man who
retains his religion, and many do so, absorbs
it as a pretext, and ultimately as a sanction
and incentive, to the "deeds done in
the body;" and out of his pious sins as
principles of action, makes a delightsome
God or Goddess who is verily himself.
The Thugs, the most pious murderers in
all India, practise their work, not without
the profit of equally pious robbery, under
the church-ritual of Siva, the goddess of
destruction; and she, being a goddess, and
being verily themselves incorporate, smiles
on her and their Thuggee, and no conscience
is evoked, and no mercy intervenes. The
victims, *testibus* the Thugs and the Goddess,
as sacrifices to her, go to heaven,—to bliss,
—and no harm is done. This is one case

of the marriage between Heaven and Hell,
between lust and religion.

67. In Genesis it is declared that "the
Sons of God saw the daughters of men
that they were fair, and they took them
wives of all which they chose." And also,
that "there were giants (Nephilim) in the
earth in those days, and especially after
that,—when the Sons of God came in unto
the daughters of man, and they bare to
them; the same became mighty men which
were of old, men of a name. And Jehovah
saw that the wickedness of man was multi-
plied on the earth, and that the fashion of
the thoughts of his heart was only evil
every day." The final destruction of the
first genus of men is here revealed. It can
now to attentive ears be rationally explained.

68. In an inspired perceptive race like
the posterity of the most ancient Church,
here in full declension and corruption, what

are the Sons of God and the fair daughters
of men, as inhabiting the same individual
and collective will ?   Do not think of them
as persons, but as influences and faculties
in a single person.   There are no persons
other than this in the first eleven chapters
of Genesis : it is *a history of Internals.*   The
Sons of God are the divine truths or
doctrinals of that Church ; these descend
directly from God into Man ; and are births
from Him.   What in distinction are the
Daughters of Men ?   They are the desires
and lusts of the same mind which receives
and contains the divine truths.   The two
unite : the doctrines entering into the lusts,
and producing systematic monsters of evil.
One mind cannot hold the two without this
gendering.   Especially under the sway of
a perverted Inspiration.   There are many
smaller instances of this extant ; and all
confirmed wickedness and breach of divine

and human laws, living in the same mind
with an acknowledged and professed religiosity, is some example of it. Murder,
pillage, inhumanity and anti-humanity, for
country and patriotism, or for humanity, is
a common form of it to-day. The daughter
of man is the lust waiting to be chosen at
free will; the son of god now is the public
pretext of its gratification in the interest of
Church and Religion.

69. The size, the Nephilim, the Gianthood,
is easily understood now. The "Son of
God" is a small internal principle in itself;
a little child in the midst, an inward voice,
a "small still voice," waiting only to be
loved and obeyed. The daughter of man
is a poor harlotry of nature demanding of
the mind to be controlled and rejected.
But put the two together in one conspiracy
of delighted consent, and a Monster of
irresistible and irreformable persuasion

comes. It comes in bigness, a devil of
divine right. Such minds, and the Most
Ancient Church at length, save the men
called Noah, consisted of nothing else, have
a stature of self-love that none can reason
with : they are as God ; and the deeper
down among them believe that they are
truly gods, that God has transfused His
divinity into them, and that there is no
longer a God in the universe. This, from
Swedenborg, is a rational account of their
self-made stature,—of the immane and the
Gigantic which is in them. The following
in his *Coronis*, n. 38, is *ad clerum*.

70. "Infernum ex illis qui ab Antiquissima
Ecclesia fuerunt, est prae omnibus aliis
infernis atrocissimum. Consistit ex illis qui
in mundo crediderunt se esse sicut Deus,
secundum dolosum effatum Serpentis (Gen.
iii. 5) ; et profundius in illo inferno sunt
illi qui sibi persuaserunt quod prorsus dii

essent, ex phantasia quod Deus Divinitatem suam transfuderit in homines, et sic quod non amplius esset Deus in universo. Ex dira illa persuasione efflatur ex illo inferno funestus putor, qui inficit vicinias tam ferali tabe ut dum aliquis approximat, occupetur primum tam lymphato delirio ut mox post singultus videatur sibi agonizare. Vidi quendam in propinquo ibi occubuisse sicut mortuus; sed translatum inde revixisse. Jacet id infernum in media plaga meridionali, circum ductum vallis, super quibus stant qui stentoriae tubae voce clamant, ' Ne accede propius.' Audivi ex angelis qui super illo inferno in coelo sunt quod cacodaemones ibi appareant sicut colubri torti in spiras inextricabiles, quod trahunt ex sublestis illorum dolis et incantationibus, quibus pellexerunt simplices ad assentiendum quod sint dii, et quod non sit Deus praeter illos.''

71. " The ancients who clothed all things in the garb of fables, by the giants who assaulted the camp of the Gods, and whom Jove struck down with his lightnings, and thrust under the fiery weight of Etna, understood these spirits, and named them Cyclops. They called their hells 'Tartara,' and 'Pools of Acheron ;' and the deeps in them 'Styx ;' and the dwellers there, ' Lernean Hydras.' "

72. Enough has been said to show how gianthood was acquired.   It is a wide theme, and the facts are exhibited all over the modern world ; but with this difference, that there is no primeval religion of inspiration to be profaned now, but the union takes place on a lower level, between the lusts of power, the scarlet woman for instance, and divine right, in ecclesiastical and political things ; neither partner to the union having any alliance with the Sons of God in Genesis ; though there is still

analogy between the two unions. Popes and Czars therefore are no bigger in stature than other people, even though Typhons of measureless self within. But in the primeval conditions, of *correspondences,* gigantic stature, monstrosity of person, was actually incubated; in cruel statures arose out of inward states. The Nephilim, and the Sons of Anak in the land of Canaan, were such. And that their progeny subsisted in the time of Moses is evident from the history in Numbers xiii. 33, where the messengers sent to explore the land reported as follows: "And there we saw the Giants, the Sons of Anak, of the Giants; and we were in our own sight as grasshoppers, and so we were in their sight."

73. This broad ground of Revelation now entered into clear reason, thus again connects itself with the Mythologies as their origin and fountain-head. The first

Giants are revealed in the Word; the later Giants are their fabulous progeny. The Greek mythology is populous with them in its earliest stages, and their characteristics tally with the Biblical stock. They are associated with the serpent myths : they are serpents as well as Giants. The Gods abolish and supersede them. The Northern Mythology also images them ; they are the first denizens of space and time through many dynasties, and are slain by Odin and Thor. Thus we observe that the savage element here as elsewhere is no crudity of prehistoric man, but a monstrous fungus sprouting out from the decay of the holy, the high and the divine.

THE DWARFS.

74. Völuspá, the Divinations of the Prophetess, tells that our first parents were originally trees, Ask and Embla ; perhaps

Ash and Elm; trees again biblically signify-
ing perceptions.   In the Persian Mythology
also man and woman come from trees as the
trunks of life: their first sensations being
also perceptions.   The dwarfs however pre-
cede mankind in the Northern Myths.   There
were many of them; and a volume might
be written concerning the correspondences
given in their names.   EDDA pronounces
strongly on the lastingness of their record.
" Their ancient pedigree shall be held in
mind as long as man's life endures."   They
were created, at first as maggots, from the
flesh and blood of Ýmir, and from his dusky
limbs; and afterwards they took on human
shapes.   We may not dwell on their tempt-
ing names; full as they are of philosophy,
and psychology.   But we select four of them
for especial consideration :

> Nordhri ok Sudhri,
> Austri ok Vestri.

In English, North, South, East, and West. They are four Atlantides supporting the four corners of the heavens : the personal *qualia* of the points of the compass ; and interesting to the spiritual man. They are indeed mere positions, and abodes of the will inside gravitation ; of the ruling love in it : thought knows as yet nothing of them, for they dwell in their own rocks and stones, and retreat into them ; and yet, though invisible, they determine the polarity of nature, and are cosmic fixations of things as they are. By position understand the quality of the things posed, and that this depends upon *positive* order. The dwarfs are therefore here the Caryatides under the natural temple. They are not mentioned in the Word as the Giants are. But East, West, North, and South are continually spoken of : they are celestial and spiritual positions, and have unvarying spiritual interpretations. In the good sense

the East signifies love to the Lord, and
regard of Him and the neighbour from that
love.   The West signifies the same love in
its setting and declension.   The South
signifies spiritual intelligence, the culmination of mental light.   The North, obscurity
of the spiritual understanding.   The ultimate
allocation of all men is determined by these
pillars of justice and judgment, and final
character is revealed and opened as the
man is carried through the climates of them.
The dwarfs are therefore of two orders ; a
light and a dark ; and the dark signify
qualities exactly opposed to the quarters
above.   " In heaven, those who constantly
turn their face to the Lord, and have their
East in Him, have the South at their right
hand, the North at their left, and the West
behind them ; and this holds howsoever they
turn."   " In the hells, the East is behind,
because they hate the Lord.   The North is

at their right because they love fallacies and
their falsities. And the South is at their
left because they spurn the light of wisdom."
(Swedenborg.) The dwarfs therefore imply
the conversion of every man to his ruling love.
They underlie all faculties : the dwarf earth
of a single generation supports the mighty
and eternal heaven : it is the footstool of the
throne, and of Him Who sits upon it. No
man notices these spiritual poles ; but all
states of individuals and communities, and
of the inner mind, point according to them.
Mythology yields them up to Revelation.
Read the Word with some knowledge,
where East, West, North, and South occur,
and you will begin to see that these specific
things are signified by them.

THE UNKNOWN AND THE UNKNOWABLE :
THE SAVAGE MEN OF THE STUDY.

75. The unknown and the unknowable lurk

at the bottom of scientist thought, and are the spectral pokers of its chaos. One or both of them is credited somehow with nature's movement and manifestation. First as to the Unknown. In a wide particular sense we must grant its existence. When a planet exhibits tractions not accounted for by the planets around it, we know that a pull is being made by another body to which these habits are due. Measuring and considering their evidence, the telescope knowingly directed sees a new planet hitherto unnoticed which balances the account. So this unknown becomes known. Here however is the material unknown of to-day, willing to be known to-morrow. But it has no relationship to the scientist unknown. There the mind sees the movement of natural things ; the graduation from the lowest up to man ; and appraises them as a serial chain ; but leaves an assumed unknown behind them; perhaps to answer for them, and certainly for itself; having no care to do more than casually recognize this unknown. The telescopes of the observatory of the unknown are in fact directed downwards and backwards, not upwards and onwards; and into each problem of perturbation, not into the primal cause of it. Thus a philosophical X stands as an inaccessible *adytum* in what ought to be Cosmic Knowledge; secretly filling it from beginning to end with unknownism or agnosticism. This unknown stands on the same ground as the Fontanellian Savage: there is no such *ens*, he, she, or it, excepting for phantasy; and if there were, its existence, as well as itself, would be unknown; worthless to talk about. And why is there no such entity? Because the Creator in the beginning of Man revealed Himself as the Word; being otherwise inscrutable, and unknown and unknowable, because dwelling in light inaccessible. He therefore completed the human mind by filling the otherwise infinite gap between Himself and the finite soul at first, and since by daily filling it; namely, with the knowledge of Himself. And so for those who will take half the trouble to understand the Word which they spend over the works, and often over their own dreams of the works, the unknown of the natural man can perish out of wisdom, then out of intelligence, and then out of science and out of sense; and become a common dock and place of sentence for other similar inventions : being thenceforth remembered as the degradation of the mind, and not as its mystery : and God manifested in Christ can take its place.

76. The Unknown belongs in part to the intellect, and in part to the will; but the Unknowable has on it the mark of special

personal dominion; being as it were an
imperial edict. It is the moral confirmation
of the Unknown, now become a determination
of persuasion. In this lower pit the ears, the
hearkening parts of wise men, are filled by
their proper fingers with egotistical wax, so
that no divine instruction shall penetrate.
The unknown may be resolved into the
known under affectionate schooling about
great circumstances; especially if there be
any rift in its absoluteness. Paul, when he
found an altar "to the unknown God," said
to the men of Athens, "Whom therefore ye
ignorantly worship, Him declare I unto you."
But this was not a wholly fantastical unknown, but the unknown God; already an
A B C and letter of authority by which
gentle willing men could begin their lesson,
and learn to read their Bible. With the
confirmed Unknowable the case is different.
Whatever any man won't know is for that

will unknowable. It bars the mind from everything but delightful picked knowledge got at by yourself and your similars. Otherwise it dwells in darkness inaccessible. Its ambition is more than the vanity of the unknown; it would procrustianize mankind. What *I* cannot know, no man can know, no man shall know, is its heart. It comprehends a whole realm and order of things which we *naturally* dislike, such dislike having debauched the will. Especially therefore a Supreme Ruler, say, the Divine Truth *revealed*, is hated as an interfering justice and judgment over life and thought. And then the hostility is extended to a Ruler of outward nature.

77. These considerations are not irrelevant to the main position of our essay; which is again, as we said above, that God's Word, Let there be light, stands at the beginning of soul, mind and faculties, and declares the

II

highest origins thoughout, as subservient to the highest purposes.

78. The unknowable defrauds us of our greatest springs of perception, and shuts the influx-gates of the genius of honest speculation against us. It locks us into cells destitute of rational furniture. The old workers with creative tools,—end, cause and effect,—belonging only to the Supreme Will here ignored, are not to hand; but only push and opportunity, the endless, causeless, and effectless dwarfs of our anti-cosmic clay. The residue of our fortune is blind nature, blind philosophy, and scientist advertisement. This again is plainly, sooner or later, the broad road through the Plagues of Egypt and the destruction in the Red Sea, to the savage man. Of him beware. He dogs the footsteps of the greatest minds, and has been the finish of the self-will and self-delusion of many proud Civilizations.

EGYPT.

79. The prechristian Myths have led
erudite men to the inference that the Incarnation is a plagiarism from Egyptian and
Indian lore; and that Egypt, spiritually the
house of bondage to Israel, is the fountain of
the ancient religions.   The History of Jesus
Christ, however, is plainly historical, and
also, as we now know, correspondential-
historical, which the Myths are not; and the
Incarnation runs through the four Gospels,
and is the seed and root of them.   Were it
not a divine as well as a natural event, the
life of Christ would no more be questioned
than the recorded birth and life of Julius
Cæsar.   And though the History be used as
a spiritual vehicle, it still stands on the
ultimate ground of fact.   Revelation has its
own way and purpose in telling things; which

is not our way. There are human ways
which illustrate it.   Drama, for instance.
The life of Julius Cæsar is presented in
Shakespeare's drama of him.   The fitting
details are woven into the Dramatic form.
No criticism exacts literality here.   Characteristic summaries, almost "correspondences"
sometimes, point the essence of the man.
And though the Drama is no continuous
photograph of his apparent existence, it
holds, according to good judges, the quality
of his real life.   That is, it gives the reader
the best idea of him.   So in a greater sense
with the Gospels as lives of Christ; they are
Revelations of His Life : and also divinely
written in Correspondences.   The Incarnation
founds these Revelations.   The common
events, of place, person, and succession, react
back ; and claim the history for the natural
world.   Egyptian myths are of no world;
they belong to neither time, place nor

person; but to astronomy perhaps, and to astrology.

80. Genesis sounds *our* first note of the Incarnation. " The seed of the woman shall bruise the serpent's head." It was the perception of the Most Ancient Church that Christ must come. This was also written in the Ancient Word, from which the first eleven chapters of Genesis are taken. For Swedenborg brings to light a divine Word antecedent to our Scriptures; but which in process of time was lost. The Book of Jasher and the Wars of Jehovah belonged to it; and are quoted in the Bible. To repeat what has already been stated (n. 24),— " The Noahtic or Ancient Church was spread through the whole of Asia; especially over Syria, Mesopotamia, Assyria, Chaldæa, the land of Canaan and its borders, Philistia, Egypt, Tyre, Sidon, Nineveh: and also over Arabia and Aethiopia; and in process of

time into Great Tartary; and thence down to the shores of the Black Sea; and over Africa. All the nations of the world have been addicted to worship under a specific religion, and no religion is possible without *a revelation* of some kind, propagated in each case from one nation to another." Egypt and India, with their two continents, were therefore at one time actual branches of the Ancient Church, and handed down the Noahtic Revelation. Their minds grew from it as their stem. They afterwards underwent spiritual defection; yet the light of that Church was their residue of life. Its Word in their memories, fragmentary indeed and perishing, became a plane of rankness and corruption for necromancers and magicians to lust in. With correspondences as tools, and spiritualisms to handle them, mythology came forth on the tablets of defaced revelation. Their Myths are therefore altered traditions of the celestial perception of the Advent of God-man as the Redeemer. Their incarnations and Avatars are collateral witnesses to this event. If the world of men was at first a tree of perceptions, a living, vibrating Yggdrasil (n. 44), it is impossible that such a seed planted as a soul in it, as that God would come into nature in the fulness of time to seek and to save, should not be a speaking life through the descendants of Adam. Every race not straightly perishing, must energize and deliver down this originally perceptive knowledge according to its own genius and hold upon nature. The minds of Egypt and India obeyed this spirit. Egypt, the representative intellect of Science, and of the square precision of sensual nature, including its religions and heathen ecclesiasticisms, obeyed its own ambitious Nile of tendency, and presented countless mythological transformations, and births and

rebirths of men and gods. And as its first
genius descended, and went towards spiritual
vastation, it laid hold of the astronomical
heaven and earth, of day and night, of sun,
moon, and constellations, to pour its inherited
persuasions through them, and to deify and
humanize them and their laws. When
Egypt thus fell down into the lusts of
magical knowledge, it came into direct
struggle with the remains of the primitive
Revelation ; and into heresy with its
Church ; and the magnitude of the strife is
shown in the hugeness of the nature which
reigned in it ; and in its unburied remains :
and its keenness is to-day seconded by the
delight with which certain of the learned
haunt its ruined history ; and oppose it to
the Gospels of Christ. This direct struggle
of Egypt and the Asiatic nations with Revelation still partially extant, gives some reason
for the crushing weight of its mythology,

compared with that of Greece, which was in no such struggle, but received the seeds of its inventions of myth from Egypt, and grew them unopposed in its own lighter ground (n. 39).

81. We cannot do justice here to the providential remainders which were still kept for Egypt; to the natural immortality of its souls : and the judgment for good, or for evil, which awaited them. The residue carefully chosen would be a little Bible for its simple sons. This is beside our scope; which is to show this mythology also as an illegitimate offspring of the Revealed Word. We only remark that excepting the practical virtue in these remainders, there is no spiritual light in them ; and that here also " the horses (understandings) of Egypt are horses of flesh and not of spirit."

82. The learned parallels between Horus and Christ, resolving the Saviour into a Solar

Myth and Gnostic hypothesis, uncover the fact, that we are here dealing with a theological question, and that such speculations are motived by a resolute denial of the Fall and the redemption of mankind as absurd and impossible.   In fact, this department of Archaeology is apt in the hands of some, like speculative scientism, to be passionately antitheological; and to recall the Apocalyptic collocation of "that City which is spiritually called Sodom and Egypt, where also the Lord was crucified."

83. The final materialism of Egypt stands out in its care for dead bodies; in its mummies animal and human : it is the typical credence of the value of the tomb, and of the resurrection of the natural carcase. Excepting its curious language and lore, the possibly recoverable genesis of its Myths, and its confirmations of the Bible, the only religious instruction to be got from it lies in

its extinction as a great human organ once. To found evolution and a modern *cultus* upon it, were to go from death to life.

84. There is then another evidence in the coincidences of Egyptian Mythology to the presence in the human soul, if no longer in a docile mind, of an expected Incarnation. The pressure of this in the old world was universal. First in the Most Ancient Church as perception. Next, in the Ancient Church as instruction : producing in time a reflected moon of light for the ancient nations. Then in the Israelitish and Jewish Word, and especially in the Prophets. All Creation groaned and travailed with it. As Bacon says, Prophecy is still to be regarded as History, but before the event : time not entering into it. So are we brooded over, in our light and in our darkness, with great coming events, and with Mercy's presentiments.

Compound Animal Forms in the Word and in Mythology.

85. Revelation, by Visions, and by waking Seership, has also brought to the mind of man composite representatives in which various beasts enter into one creature, forming compound animals; and others in which man and animal are conjoined. The Prophets and the Apocalypse present many instances of this. All these are rationally and spiritually significative when their meaning is revealed. To enumerate them would require a volume. They belong to the internal sense of the Word; and they have attestation in human nature; for the qualities of men are sometimes discerned as those of specific animals, and a single man may have several such animals in his character; a Shakespeare or a Browning

might poetize him with the head and face
of one beast, with the breast of another, and
with the limbs and claws of a third; and
painters might truly colour him so. Horace
puts man together organ-wise in this very
fashion. Dēmos is commonly known as a
many - headed monster. This comes of
Revelation, deeply agent in the causal
recesses of the human soul and personality.
The emblems and insignia which nations
apply to themselves attest the same thing:
the double-headed Eagle, and the like. To
say nothing of the great traditional mirror
of Heraldry. The learned can supply such
facts in great variety. But a reflex of them
exists in Mythology as a derivative from
Revelation. The Indian Myths are full of
these compound creatures. They were
sculptured in ancient Assyria, where we
have the human-headed bulls; and the
Sphinx leads off an abounding line of such

hieroglyphs in Egypt. The Centaur occurs among the Greek Myths. All these have grounds and reasons in heathen man. It is however in the spiritual world and its divine ground that they find their original and their justification. There the Cherubs are full of eyes before and behind. This plasticity of forms so fixed to us is a devolution from a Power Who makes and unmakes forms at will in creative right and might to express Himself in the Logos. With Him all things are Words of the Word, and the language is infinite in its imagery, and the images are bodies of real creation. The living combinations too are endless, and exist among the people to whom they correspond. It is not expedient to dwell further on this theme. Swedenborg has treated it fully : see his *Apocalypse Revealed.* The rational mind can there be instructed about it ; and learn the necessity

of these divine appearances, and the meaning of each spiritual form. " The earth hath
bubbles as the water hath," as Shakespeare
says of the witches in *Macbeth*. These
forms are exhalations of the spiritual earths
in correspondence with their societies, and
are prophetic of their futures.

86. For the most part on the evil side
the forms are monstrous, and embody the
persuasions and dogmas of false religions,
which make the composite mind into the
various shapes portrayed : for such persuasions and dogmas confirmed are spiritually
constructive and organic, although churches
and societies here have no conception
of the strange beasts they are living
in. They are especially representative of
and correspondent to false principles; the
Dragon in the Apocalypse, for instance,
embodies the cardinal heresy of justification
by faith alone, and the clergy who are

in this creed confirmed are its organic monads.

87. Such forms occur chiefly in the Prophets and in the Apocalypse, and not in the earlier books of the Word. But the spiritual world contains them ; and therefore they are represented in Mythology, all of which is post-revelational. The human mind wills, thinks, and engenders and produces, in the current of the spiritual downrush to which it has yielded itself, or opened the door. Here it may be remarked that the age and date of the several books of the Bible as criticism deals with them, is of no importance to these subjects : whether Moses, or who, wrote the Five Books, matters not. They stand on the internal sense. And they embody the most ancient correspondences gathered up by Cain, and then by Enoch, and hand down in a divinely-inspired Word the perceptive Church of the earliest mankind.

The Age of Myths is past.

88. There are reasons why these things have been kept. One is that they could not in their degraded and hideous forms be wrenched from the sensual man, without doing violence to his nature. They are the children of his life and *proprium*. Another reason is, not merely that they corroborate Scripture, — the Word, — but that the science of correspondences now restored, will ultimately teach the meaning of them to all races, and so help to win them back by their own memorial archives and traditions to Christ, to Whom all correspondences converge, and in Whom all myths disappear. Who thus also shall bruise the Serpent's head.

A Mode of Origin of Myths.

89. A word of surmise on the immediate origin of myths considered as new points

I

of departure; namely, on their mode of origin. The history of spiritual-mental states, veritably, the Theological History given by Swedenborg, makes the divine origin of correspondences plain. Read through carefully the First Volume of his *Arcana Cœlestia* to be apprised of this fact. Every instructor of the people now, every well-meaning and enlightened Journalist, especially the very gifted Editor of the *St. James's Gazette*, ought to be acquainted with it. He will find in it a clear resuscitation for our knowledge and benefit of races in long succession and series which have passed away, but which were the youngest and eldest children of Jehovah God; and of their love and its now incomprehensible Wisdom. This great Palimpsest of obliteration and recovery, is for our reading, that we may live again into the Word. Let me tell that learned man that these Revelations also shed a supreme light upon Society and Politics, because they show from an imperturbable divine standpoint what human nature really is.

The Origin of Correspondences in the Adamic Men.

90. The knowledge of correspondences was given in the regenerated life, not of the race of Adam, but of the race named Adam; the race of Adam was a declension. These earliest men in the proper sense of Man, were the earliest, the celestial, Church. Adam gave things—they came to him—their names, and Jehovah, who inspired him, accepted his nomenclature. And by perception from his Creator and Maker he possessed the meaning of things in this world of forms, as corresponding to spiritual things; and in expressing the spiritual things, the natural things were the names

that flowed from them and fitted them. Of course as common sense is not excluded by, but is the base and support of, spiritual sense, so also for the race named Adam, in handling natural things and their uses and functions (which made them into correspondences), the series of expressions was different, and did not proceed from the inmost where Jehovah was, but through space and time, from one natural thing to another, in a very practical daily life, through marriage, human companionship, and the sweetness of natural light and duty. Language itself was doubtless given on these two planes.

Adam and Eve, the Proprium.

91. He, therefore, this supreme race, this " Adam which was the Son of God," spoke by Creations, and the Word which was with him spoke by the same. All these

earliest generations were called by single proper names, as marking that every Society whether on earth or in heaven is one man. In this presiding divine Word the serpent was the sensual nature, harmless, benign and all-fruitful in its place, and Eve was the Selfhood, *the amour propre*, what Sweden-borg calls *the Proprium.* There was nothing "ignorant" or "savage," but some-thing divinely lovely, powerful and beautiful in speaking as God and His Word speak, by creations. When the mode of speech sprang from within, it gave the sense that spiritual *states* of love and wisdom were being created. And divine and human converse was active with true substances building the temple of life. This speech was different to our words and letters, which of themselves are intrinsically unmeaning. It was a human body of speech, having in it the heart of the men of the golden years, and heaven and earth reciprocally engendered in it. In hushes of expression it could express volumes as Genesis and the Apocalypse express them to souls.

INSPIRATION BY AND REVELATION FROM JEHOVAH GOD BEGAN ALL TRUE MANHOOD.

92. Revelations were thus the beginning, for man with his freewill had to be raised from the dust of the ground, from the "preadamite" man, *homo protoplastus*, as Swedenborg calls him,—not from the pre-historic man,—into the Church called Adam. Nothing else could be initiatory to a perfectly helpless creature like man just made, but God alone. In defect of natural father and mother, God and His particular ministering spirits [1] of course tended him, and

---

[1] "Let us make man in our own image:" the plural form here refers to "the ministry of men-angels." See Swedenborg on Genesis,

were themselves his unknown circumstances.
The ultimate Revealer, the First and the
Last, Who was and Who is and Who is
to come, was in the background, accom-
modate by appearances stage by stage to
every the minutest state of the creature who
was to be first his Image, and then his
Likeness and Vicegerent. And so by incessant Revelations, divine as the bosom
of God, and more tenderly natural than the
mother's breast, and by their instructions,
and by implicit following and obedience, out
of the man made from dust, the Adam Man
was born. Visions and dreams, those
earliest and least intrusive of helps to
the pure and unsuperstitious, were also
attendant instructors sent from heaven;
for in the innocent perpetual advance of
man's spiritual state to its culmination in

chap. i. ver. 26, in *Arcana Cœlestia*, n. 50. *N.B.*—All angels have
risen from the ranks, or in other words, have once been men.

the celestial state, no impurity of hereditary evil and falsity could spoil or deflect the influx, or lay hold of it, as would be the case at the present day with the most of men, for personal ends.

93. If man from a mere shape and shell of humanity became a living soul from the inbreathing or inspiration of the breath of God into his nostrils, it is clear to reason that the inspiration was continued in every direction necessary to endow the creature in compliance with his own God-given faculties, and to lead him and her into life. This has become an intellectual fact after being revealed as an indispensable work of the divine providence in the *Arcana Cœlestia* of Swedenborg.

DECLENSIONS PERPETUAL.

94. The primitive mind was thus charged with supernal and angelic influences; and

to a great extent received them consciously, and conversed with angels in the language of correspondences, in which also the First Word was written, and in which our Old and New Testaments accordingly are also written. But this state of perception did not continue. The stages of its decline, to its end, are written in Genesis. But this is not the place to dwell upon them further. Suffice it to say that from the earliest times the human mind was stored with a multitude of correspondences which had been mighty as actual powers in the past, and it still had some use and abuse of them. But as the Adamic ages closed up like a scroll, the unity which reigned in them and over them, the unity of God was lost, and the objects of nature which embodied the correspondences, or certain presumed regents and spirits of nature, were worshipped. But with varying degrees

of grossness.   The powers of the mind, the
events of life and time, and the departments of nature,—the Sun, Moon and Stars,
—thus had gods assigned to them.   It was
a perfectly consequent and so to speak
natural result of the degradation of a perceptive church : embodied false perceptions,
real hallucinations of the then powerful
religious influx, were the issues.   This
disintegrating end may have occurred
rapidly, on the *facilis descensus* principle,
for the ages of the patriarchs do not signify
periods, but like all biblical numbers, they
are *states of life.*

RESTORATIONS PERPETUAL BY AND FROM THE DIVINE : SUCCESSIVE CHURCHES.

95. A stream of new human *propria* evoked
and inspired, was however continued through
the medium of New Dispensations, and in the

Church after the Flood, perception was lost,
and a new organon, of conscience, before
uncreated, because perception superseded it,
was given to Mankind. A new human
centre and nature signified by the Church
named of Noah. This also was destroyed in
successive generations of lapsing heredities.
In distinction from the Adamic Church this
was a spiritual Church, with external truth,
not internal love, for a centre: truth communicated not to inspired people, but to
an instructable conscience by an external
inspired or Divine Word. A third point
of divine departure was a natural Church,
the Israelitish, in which the natural good
and truth of life were enjoined and preserved.
Correspondences were still possessed by and
taught in this third dispensation. The
Jewish Church, a continuation of this, was
a merely ritual or representative Church,
which possessed neither perception, nor

conscience, nor natural good, as centres, but its mission was obedience to the Ten Commandments, and representation in rites and forms of the correspondences in the Jewish Word, on which the remaining communication of heaven with man was founded.

HEATHEN RELIGIONS AT THE SIDE: THEIR WAYS AND MEANS.

96. Alongside this great highway of Providences, the Churches which were its stations sent out as they declined roads of heresies, and ultimately institutions of idolatries, in which the Word of Jehovah was perverted and abused. These are the Heathen Religions. And here specially Mythologies and False Words and Worships originated, not from naked Celts, or skin-clad cave or lake-dwellers, but from the lovers of empire on its first and highest

thrones, seeking assistance, like Macbeth with the witches, at the cauldrons of self love from magical influx. In no sense divine Revelations, they were remainders in the wreck after the three disastrous voyages of self-made humanity. Still they were of the nature of food, these relics of the science of correspondences. In Greece,[1] and possibly in Asia and in Egypt, these correspondences were draped afresh, clothed with the flesh of those races, and

[1] "Apollo's oracle at Delphi was one of the most celebrated in Greece. Delphi, which is in Phocis, was situated on the slopes of Mount Parnassus, and was originally called Pytho [the Serpent]. In the centre of the temple dedicated to Apollo was a small opening in the ground, from which mephitic exhalations rose from time to time. When the oracle was to be consulted, a priestess, called Pythia, [of the serpent again,] was placed upon a tripod, or three-footed seat or table, which stood over the chasm. All the words she uttered while intoxicated by the vapours were supposed to contain revelations from Apollo, and were carefully noted down, converted into verse by a poet employed for the purpose, and communicated by the priests to the people. . . . The temple at Delphi was the depository of immense riches, the offerings of kings and private persons who had received favourable answers from the oracle." (*A Smaller Classical Mythology*, p. 77. Edited by Dr. William Smith, 1882.)

with poetry and myth.   Another factor
supervened, a busy and a common one—
our old acquaintance, even—Spiritism.   It
was a mimicry of the primeval revelations.
These were converse with God and His
Angels; but this new appetite of man was
for necromancy; for questioning the fates,
and learning the ultimate upshot of things
from dead ancestors.

97. Spiritism as it exists at this day
has thus a use for the New Church in
the light it sheds upon what happens to
the human mind at the end of Churches;
when one section of those who are vastated
of religious truth goes to Atheism, and
another section proceeds to make a new
religion for itself with the worship of the
common man, now called "Humanity,"
for its Cult.   The boldest part of the
latter host goes to Spiritism; hopes and
fears and dreams of good in it; and gives

forth relations of the spirit-world from its
own familiars. These stories are not mythologies now, because the science of correspondences is not extant among the familiar
spirits. They are presumed interviews with
the departed on the old lines of space
and time, matter and person; for the most
part flatteries of infidelity, and denials of
spiritual consequences in favour of the world
and the flesh. They are opiates and in-
toxicants, and eminently persuasions. But
nevertheless they are illustrations of what
would be correspondence in a former age;
and of the magical mode of it.

98. Without taking note of spiritism,
which where it is not a mortal imposture
is a power, though often an infernal one,
it would be difficult at this day to
understand the mode of production of the
mythologies, or to see them in any connected series with other religious events.

Undoubtedly, they belong by telegraph and telephone to the Ancient Magic, and sit upon its oracular stools. Emperors also still consult the mediums. The Pythoness, the Serpent-woman, attests in her name the old worship of the serpent, whose seducing voice was the earliest word uttered from below.

Uses of Mythologies as Schoolmasters and Art-Masters in Language and Æsthetics.

99. But let it not be forgotten, as we remarked in the beginning, that the Greek Myths, of the Divine Providence, were received out of the spiritual world into a literature young, strong, and destined to endure for what we may call, "all time;" a literature that like a Church was a new departure in the culture of mankind; that the myths were purged and beautified in it; and that the pythonesses lost their hoarse-

ness as their oracles were re-echoed through the Poetry of Greece, and reflected from the walls and vaults of its Temples. "Forward stept the perfect Greek," says Emerson. And Myth partook of his step through epic, drama, sculpture and architecture, and became an admissible thread for illustration and beauty in all even Christian literature. The Word had presently to be translated for the whole world, and language in its more modern life was thus distilled from Hybla and Parnassus, to sweeten and ennoble it for its sacred work.

100. There were here two subordinate inspirations at work. First, the Delphic Mediumship in its rugged possibilities. This uttered the old heathen gods afresh, and as is usual with mediumship, altered them in names of qualities to the Greek temperament and exaction, early and late; so that here we have an old pressure or tradition, and a new starting point.

K

Secondly, a band of poets standing around the tripods, and down the historic series; receiving, handing on, and finally bringing up, the myth-offspring. Another new imprint. These poets, the first purely human art-creators, had in them from the spiritual side, and also from a real mission which impelled them, a more than Promethean Genius. Looking at them as the primitive novelists of the myths, they could not but mould and temper them in the interest of art and beauty; and give them a stamp and a shape suitable for currency in the universal literary mind.

PRIMEVAL PERCEPTION AND ITS STREAMS OF MEMORY AND TRADITION.

101. There are then two ways and two series. There is perception, for the *earliest* races, of true correspondences: tradition,

memory and memorial of such correspondences for the *early* races; dictation
of divine messages in correspondences to
the Israelites and the Jews; the Gospels
and the Apocalypse written in correspondences to the Christian Church. And
now a full revelation of what the correspondences are and signify in the
commissioned writings of Swedenborg.
This is the direct series, attesting the
divinity of the Word. The collateral
human series is the Mythologies. In their
antecedents and accompaniments, these
Mythologies signify and involve powerful
nations and states of mind; huge emanci-
pations from the order of heaven; exalta-
tions of human genius; poetry; imagination
and fancy corresponding : serpentine science,
vast, hissing and erect; the birth of
pyramids and colossal architectures; earth-
dominating and heaven-scaling ambitions,

national and individual; and still, above them, and within, written in the laws of their nature, and on the walls of it, fluent traces of the ancient correspondences coming sideways and askance. Add to this that all these heathen races had the pressure of their ancestors by magnetic co-heredity above them; and then add Spirit-Mediumship; and it will be evident that Mythology came from many and great Factors. Also that every piece of it is an end and not a beginning: a *cul de sac* of human nature, and at no time a philosophy for it, or any struggle after a philosophy.

102. It is indeed well that correspondential mythology is now barren so far as propagation is concerned. Its creations are too lasting where rapid perishability and cremation are the better end. Even where it falls into nursery tales, it survives one scientific hypothesis of the world after

another. Jack the Giant-Killer, a son of old Thor, and a functional relation of Jove, who was also a Giant-Killer, has a longer lease in him than Modern Thought, and is in possession on its merits. It is a gracious circumstance that our *illustrissimi* are ephemeral; that their scientisms are not communicated by mediums on tripods, but by the passing learned; that they have "short sentences," and escape out of the pillories of time by the bills of mortality. But mythology is not transitory thus.

THE REMAINDERS OF THE HEATHENISMS.

103. Following the series of the Churches indicated above, it may be clear that each of them has left its own particular ruins behind it; its heathen remainders and desolations. The Serpent-worship extant still, and once in power all over the gentile

world, is one record of the destroyed
Adamic or celestial Church, the most ancient
of the churches. The heathenisms of
Babylon and Assyria and of the nations of
Canaan ; also of Egypt, and finally of
Greece and Rome, are the fragments and
perverted correspondences of the Ancient,
Noahtic, or spiritual Church ; and of the
memories of the Israelitish or natural
Church : these have vast branches still
subsisting as diverse heathenisms in the
great East and its islands. Lastly, the
Jews are the Jews, themselves the fossils of
the Jewish Church. Old Clothes, not disre-
spectfully, but spiritually spoken, are their
mythology. The same inevitable consequences of doctrinal and religious apostasy
and decline are extant in the Christian
Church. Though it has no mythology, it
has Dogmas which correspond. Its
plurality of divine persons ; its finite human

passions in the Allfather, interpretable away from their grossness by no law of correspondences, as Jehovah is interpretable all through the Word of the Old Testament; the Son, the dispenser of indulgences for all lives through faith alone in His imputed Merits : these are truly the final fables of the first Christian Church, though the word, Christian, rescues it from the denomination of heathenism ; because it has pleased the Lord to plant in its very place a New Christian Church.

ETHNOLOGIC - GEOGRAPHICAL LIGHT WILL COME OF THE BIBLICAL REVELATION OF THE CHURCHES.

104. It is credible that with these divine informations from the Word regarding the successive Churches, the history of Idolatry and Myth will be written afresh, so that the

various Mythologies may be allocated to the
true centres of which they are the deflexions
and corruptions, and of which at first they
were the profanations. This however is a
matter for the more learned to undertake.
The New Church will have its keen-sighted
explorers who will dig in these mounds, and
unearth their monuments. Fresh evidence
will probably be found there of the geographical distribution of races, particularly
with regard to their extension and outward
migration from a common centre; myths,
where they still occur, being the signposts
backwards and forwards; pointing from the
land of Canaan to Africa; and from the
Mexican and the Peruvian to the Polynesian
and the Esquimaux. For at first sight it is
not feasible that the members of the human
family, created as we now know indisputably
for a primeval Eden which they inhabited
and tasted, were driven by anything but the

compulsive fact of a declining spiritual life, and force from without, *vis major*, put upon it, to Finland or Greenland or Western Africa, or the remote islands of the sea. But this subject in its pursuit belongs to another time and place.

105. Finally we may see that the concentric waves of correspondential mythology are exhausted in their last force and representation in the *state* of the whole of the savage tribes. They are the terminal sand of the human sea; the kronic ends of atheism and self-development in life and mind, typical self-made men; and exhibitions of such. Ages of destructive passions and revenges, of unbrotherly collidings, ages of lusts, and of glory, have gone before in terrible logic, and gendered these remains of human forms and faculties; which now, as Sir John Lubbock well says, demand our brotherly care. They belong to Allfather with a

second helplessness the opposite of the first.
They die out here. But there is another
world for the good among them after this
one; conscience is inextinguishable in them;
and there, through tutelage appointed by the
Divine mercy and its wisdom, they will be
raised towards Man again, and find their
own room in the house of many mansions :
all good States and Kingdoms helping them
so long as they are here.

ATTESTATIONS FROM THE WORD. NEBU-
   CHADNEZZAR'S DREAM OF THE IMAGE.
   DANIEL'S VISION OF THE DIVINE RE-
   STORER.

106. The great drama of divine-human
history here indicated, from the Man Adam
to the savage man, is written down in
Nebuchadnezzar's dream as divined by the
Prophet Daniel.

107. " Thou, O king, sawest, and behold a great image. This image, which was mighty, and whose brightness was excellent, stood before thee; and the aspect thereof was terrible. As for this image, his head was of fine gold, his breast and his arms of silver, his belly and his thighs of brass, his legs of iron, his feet part of iron, and part of clay. Thou sawest till that a stone was cut out without hands, which smote the image upon his feet that were of iron and clay, and brake them in pieces. Then was the iron, the clay, the brass, the silver and the gold, broken in pieces together, and became like the chaff of the summer threshing-floors ; and the wind carried them away, that no place was found for them ; and the stone that smote the image became a great mountain, and filled the whole earth." Daniel, chap. ii. 31–36.

108. Also further : the ultimate end achieved for mankind by the incarnation is as follows.

109. "I saw in the night visions, and, behold there came with the clouds of heaven one like unto a son of man, and he came even to the Ancient of Days, and they brought him near before him. And there was given unto him dominion, and glory, and a kingdom, that all the peoples, nations, and languages should serve him : his dominion is an ever-lasting dominion, which shall not pass away, and his kingdom that which shall not be destroyed." Daniel, chap. vii. 13, 14.

Divine History and Human History.

110. History is twofold, Human and Divine. Human History tells what man-kind has done, and what its outward fates have been. Divine History tells what mankind itself was and is, and records its several dooms. The persons of prominent men in space and time are the subject of the

historian, always with some reference, often a slender one, to the people of whom they were the chiefs. This department is a superficial romance, indispensable to be well told. But divine History tells of the fates of all souls in their collective capacity, and of the Spiritual Judgment upon them in this collective, and in their individual, capacity also. The Word, the Logos, is the sole resort of this latter history. Its annals are the record, infinite in detail, of the inheritances of good and evil, and the consequences of each.

THERE IS NO SUCH THING AS PRE-HISTORIC MAN, AND NO SUCH MAN AS THE FONTANELLIAN SAVAGE.

111. Taking the writings of Swedenborg for what they are, a historical Revelation of the states of humanity from the beginning

to this day; and onwards; for it rounds in with the whole future,—a Revelation of the First and of the Second Adam,—it is clear that, spiritually, there are no prehistoric times so far as mankind is concerned; for ages preparatory for man are ages of moving matter and life, and though (in time) before history whether sacred or profane, they are incommensurate with history, and cannot be named of it. They are simply unhistoric and ante-human; that is, there are no men or women in them. The Lord God has written the history of the Man who is the one subject of history, and "let there be light" (from Him, obviously Divine Light), is the dawn and the seed of it. Before this there is *homo protoplastus;* recorded, yet scarcely historic; the clay awaiting the potter: "the earth waste and void, and darkness upon the face of the deep." And every man by creation and birth is in a lower sense *homo protoplastus* at first. But all that can be known of man's primal history is known from the extended and detailed internal sense of Scripture now unlocked; the divine cypher in which it is written has been opened both in the spiritual and natural worlds, as was needful, to Swedenborg.[1] Thus our brethren, for such they were and are; the lake-dwellers and the cave-men; "the troglodytes, pile-villagers, and bog-people," as Virschow calls them; who contended with the abundance of wild beasts for a dole of nature, occupy so to speak no period in annals. They are neither of primal history, which is Divine, nor of secondary history, which is human; not prehistoric but post-historic; the cessa-

---

[1] I desire to recommend to the reader's attentive perusal, *The Garden of Eden*, a little book by the Rev. John Doughty, procurable from James Speirs, 36 Bloomsbury St., London, W.C. It is a popular but adequate statement of the doctrine-history of the Most Ancient Church, and will materially assist as a first book towards the understanding of the early chapters of Genesis.

tions, ends and extinctions of History : undynastical dust: the impotent ends of sex and genesis. Also they were hunted creatures, *aboriginal nowhere.* And on the upward road they lead nowhere. Body and flesh, albeit alive and for their hour propagating, are destinies for museums, and subjects of natural history. Scientism has its own views in making much of their bones. Science dealing with facts alone, and not insurgent against its better self, is, however, of great use and profit. A strong divinity shapes its ends. Dispossessed of unseemly hypotheses, it attests biblical truth in its exhibition of these earth-born children ; the lowest evidences of the height and depth of the Fall. But like buildings and temples once, now worn down to " the ground from which they were taken," science has a monopoly of them, and is the common grave and respectful mound of such lost tribes.

MAN'S EPOCH, AND WHEN HE WAS PUT INTO
NATURAL CREATION.

112. What is the relation of the foregoing
facts to the Geological record? Genesis,
chapters i. and ii., deals neither with Geo-
genesis nor with Geology, but with the first
human will and understanding ; with Adam
or Man. This is proved and known, and
to those who recognize it, there is no contest
between Revelation on this head, and
modern knowledge. The *antiquity of man*,
the epoch in which he first appeared on the
material scene, is out of the direct scope of
the informations of Heaven. Science has
exclusive possession of the question at
present. Eden, indeed, and the garden
planted eastward in it by the Lord God,
implies a place, possibly related to the
four rivers which correspondentially went

out from it; a place, because man was
always a man, and was created in space and
time; and therefore his first abode both for
revelation and reason is in some sort a
geographical reality. As to time and its
antiquity, what years meant then is not
revealed, or otherwise ascertained; the
successive curves in the spiral of time are
unknown quantities; but successive states
of man, the relations of his will and
understanding to his Creator and Maker,
are instead of times, and also of spaces, in
the Word; these periods and places are
human, and heavenly, and not astronomical,
or geographical; and now are known. Yet
some parts beyond conjecture have visible
faces, and faith and reason are the two eyes
that see them. Man appeared upon earth
when a motherly spot was ready for him;
when there was a proper environment. He
was no playmate or plaything of ichthyosaurus

and plesiosaurus. In the measured cooling of time and space, at length an Eden climate was exactly reached ; a balmy centre capable of a garden and a home in it worthy of God and His infants. A pleasant spot designate, as our Tyndall might grant, in the willing bosom of the sun. The growing and living creatures in that area were suitable and amenable. The first sons and daughters of God, one or many, babies, or adults ; in any case, the youngest always, though now reckoned the oldest humanity ; did not pass their heart's babyhood, its infancy, or its nursery days, among cave-bears and hairy rhinoceroses : the cradle and early walks of Allfather's children were watched and accompanied by better maids than these. Also we know nothing of their natural sepulture ; nothing of their bones, which perchance were not ossified and not fossilizeable like ours. The bones called

prehistoric are none of theirs. *Noscuntur
a sociis.* These latter bones are of recent
savages contemporary with evil beasts.
Such details, however, have nothing to do
except inferentially with the downright
Word of Genesis. It deals with the first
religion, which is necessarily the first Man.
But these things may flow as approximate
streams of clear common sense from its truths.

113. Among the foremost defenders of the
sacredness and validity of Genesis[1] stands
the name of the late Thomas Karr Callard,
F.G.S., an indefatigable explorer of whatever

---

[1] The controversy about Genesis as with reservations a literal
account of the Creation enlists great names *pro* and *con.* We
must hope that the Spiritual Sense honestly studied in Swedenborg's
Arcana Cœlestia may decide the question on a higher ground.
Such a study is worthy of the genius of a Huxley. The difficulty
for the scientific man lies in admitting that there is a Word of
God in the case. Let him then try it as a hypothesis. The
difficulty for the believer lies in opening his mind to perceive
that the Word must have divine contents not visible in the
letter ; and that the justification of the Bible rests on these.
Read also Swedenborg's *Apocalypse Revealed,* for ample materials
for forming a judgment on the whole subject.

belongs to the so-called "prehistoric man."
His treatises are of importance from the
doubt they cast on the human origin of many
of the celts and edged flints of which so much
capital of antiquity has been made : out of
which indeed has been conjured up the
geologist's Frankenstein, the Palæolithic
man, whom T. K. Callard has probably put
to his final rest. See his pamphlet, *The
Geological Evidences of the Antiquity of
Man reconsidered*, 1875. He travelled far
and wide in the interest of his Bible, and
brought a mine of experience to bear on his
special subject. The views in this paper
are not indeed his ; but the purpose of
both is the same : to derive from Genesis
an undeniable account of God's Creation,
which account obviously God alone can give.
And if, as we hold, Genesis gives a divine
account of all spiritual creation, it would be
difficult to decline the possibility that light

must come from thence illustrating natural creation. Not indeed the external and so - called material events presumed by Astronomy, and the planetary changes unearthed by Geology, which are not creation, but formation and arrangement subsequent; but the divine process which like a soul informs and underlies and builds up the body of every world; as the human soul builds up by ends and causes of God's own in it, its human form and body as its effect. This is creation and divine architecture; and except by Swedenborg it is a realm of real creation which has been entered by no man. See his Work, *The Worship and Love of God.*

114. "Dean Stanley," remarks Mr. Callard, "says of the earlier Biblical records, that they were not, and could not be, literal and prosaic matter-of-fact descriptions of the beginning of the world, of which, as

of its end, no man knoweth, or can conceive, except by figure and parable." "If
we were prepared," Mr. Callard says, "to
accept the teaching of the earlier Biblical
records as simply teaching by figure and
parable, we should still expect that these
figures and parables should be the embodi-
ments of truths, or else they would be to
us worse than useless. But it would be
very difficult to find any figurative or parabolical meaning in these early records that
would harmonize with the teaching concerning the Antiquity of Man. What meaning,
for example, was intended to be conveyed
by those Biblical records, when they say that
'God created man in His own image'?
Surely *Palæolithic* man was not created in
the image of God ; the image of the lowest
savage, just one remove from the brute, was
all that was impressed upon him. What
again could have been the parabolical teach-

ing of the *fall* of man? Surely there was no room for Palæolithic man to fall." (T. K. Callard, in the preface to *op. cit., supra.*) From which it appears that this pious and thoughtful writer rejected the idea that the Man or Adam of Genesis was in any way identical or contemporaneous with the hypothetical prehistoric man of the scientists. Dean Stanley also rightly divined that creation could be imaged forth by figure and parable; which was the nearest thing he could say to the embodiment of its truths in correspondences.

THE CONDITIONS ON WHICH ADAM WAS ADAM, AND IN THE GARDEN EASTWARD IN EDEN. ALSO EMBRYOLOGICAL CONSIDERATIONS. PALÆONTOLOGY FINDS MONSTERS, BUT NOT EVIL MONSTERS.

115. We may further conceive rationally that this prime estate, depending upon the

relation of Jehovah to the selfhood or *pro-prium* with freewill as its determinant, was, like the conscience and the spiritual and moral natures, now a perishable state ; and that when the first Adam, the living soul, was insurgent, and disobedient to the heavenly influx, the primitive personality was defaced, perhaps rapidly, the fall standing only one chapter away from the perfected creation. Thereby the order of things was essentially changed, because man, the end and summit, changed himself, and was changed. The inspirations in him, in a world still of correspondences, became a new and vast creation around him. The earth was cursed for his sake, and it yielded thorns and thistles. The creatures which were fœtal in nature, the huge animals that were feeders of it with life, the realm of fossils now, gave place to another order of creations of malign intent, which had man-kind not for their end and crown, but for

their prey. The earlier forms separated
from their epoch, the colossal mammoths and
lizards, look shocking and ugly indeed, but
yet not more so than the fœtal forms of all
animals, which are repulsive, and not meant
to be gazed upon unless by scientific eyes.
But notwithstanding this, the early evolutions
out of the fervid waters and the steaming
earth, which in the letter are commanded to
bring forth beast, bird and creeping thing,
the Deinotheria, Iguanodons, Pterydactyla,
and all the brood, were not inimical to man,
for man was not in their days. They were
Ymirs (see n. 41) in preparatory nature,
introducing into it a needful influx of life.
(See the chapter, " Man's Place in Nature "
in the Author's work on *Human Science and
Divine Revelation,* where " *Zoï-Statics* " are
treated of.) These teeming monsters preyed
indeed upon each other, in which regard the
human fœtus also is an example. It contains

many organs and channels of organism which are indispensable to it, and are its state, and these are consumed for the permanent ones by advancing exigencies of life. Other and ultimately higher functions eat them up and destroy them. These deciduous parts are the human organization tending to birth and preparing for it. They die out; perhaps destroy each other because they have served their turn in the torrid womb, and fulfilled their work. The lasting organs clearly feed upon them. Nay, does not the human embryo also live upon human food, and consume the willing fortunate mother ? But evil beasts are not of this order, but come out of perverse man, are images of him, and associate with him on equal terms when at last he grounds in the savage state.

116. Spermatozoa are examples of the forms that may occur in the human initia-ments themselves; serpentine forms; and

similar cases of monstrose appearance will readily suggest themselves to the students of embryology. Such forms are however in the direct lineage of the physical man. They tend to humanity. But when the whole creation was in embryo, the to us strange evolutions of life were preparatory to man, and ended with themselves, breeding no successors. They were the vitals of the then world, without which it would have been dead animally. It is not wonderful that we do not understand their forms, since science has no imagination of their preparatory functions in the world-organism. The religious mind which has not studied these things, may easily be led to suppose that the " poor monsters" disinterred were evil beasts because to it they are ugly ; and so may be led to grant evil before man, and find it difficult to believe in a primitive Eden : or to follow the Word where it says, "And God saw all that

He had made, and behold it was very good."

117. There is also another consideration derived from common experience to be alleged for monstrous and colossal forms; namely, from Arts and Inventions; which are the human types of creations. The killing of Giants has humane significance here. As a rule, the progress of invention in the mind and its works in nature, is from the great to the small, from the unwieldy to the shapely. Trace any perfected machine through its developments to what it at length becomes, and you find so much put aside, so much simplicity put on, so much handiness got at the expense of weight and complexity; so much compactness and tendency to smallness, not littleness, attained. The machine may be said to feed on its early stages and to absorb them. If the trial of them had not been gone through, it could not have reached

the final elegance of its use. It was a monster at first, having decorum of perfection constantly in view : this being at length gained by elimination and rejection. Divine creation in this respect seems to be similar to human creation. So also, age by age, each last century is worked off into an exiguous remainder which stands for the purpose of the lives and works now in hand. We do not find in this scheme that the lowest form budges from its place ; it is reproduced on its own level by a more advanced creation, which is the lowest still. *E.g.* a font of types is at the bottom now where it was with Caxton, and never becomes a cerebrum.

118. These indeed are sidelong considerations, though they may be suggested by what is directly revealed on the "golden tables" of the Word. Science thus perhaps, ignoring the savage man as an origin, and

looking at Geology and Palæontology, and then at survivals and Natural History, through the lens of the spiritual Genesis, may see further into the natural Genesis than is possible with her present optical means.

HEREDITIES DIE OUT IN THE SAVAGE MAN.

119. According to our good old friend, Herbert Spencer, "Out of Savages unable to count up to the number of their fingers, and speaking a language containing only nouns and verbs, arise at length our Newtons and Shakespeares." This occurs, he opines, by the increment of passive and active habits and faculties represented continually in fresh brain structures and combinations, and transmitted hereditarily to new generations of similar accumulators; each age tending to stand upon the shoulders of the last, till the flint implement

becomes a rifled cannon, and the imitative "bow-wow," a Macbeth and a Hamlet. We do not find *that* sequence in things, or these amplifications from savage cerebrums. On the contrary, nothing is more distinctive of the savage man than decay of Nature,—than the dying out of his heredities; and we may safely infer from this, the obliteration of much of the complex mechanism of his brains. He is thus thriftless to the fortunes of his forefathers, and his only increment is increased loss of natural parts; often attended however with a development of the sense of outward spheres of distance, smells, and the like, as a transient compensation. This privilege approximates him to the instinctive animals. By degradations or natural vices and "vastations" it would be conceivable that a Newton or Shakespeare line of men should become savages; but the reverse process is impossible. The reason is mental and cerebral. The savage loses ancestry by parting with ancestral qualities one by one, and with their nerve and brain correspondents. Whether his head becomes measurably smaller or not is a question; but that the contents of his skull grow more and more worthless for transmitting quality, is beyond dispute. His inherited life dwindles until he has no past and no future; no common but only a single private memory, and he is a waif and stray of an hour, a foundling: a denatured eggless butterfly going back through a caterpillar and ending in a stone. As we read him, he parts with his heredities one after another as the pages of a volume, until nothing but the blank leaves at the beginning and the end of him, are left. In these conditions, in permanence of nature he is below the beasts; a fact which differences him for ever from the animal tribes, from the ascidian to the elephant. Their instincts are

M

indestructible, and cannot be lost, though they are superficially altered by circumstances, and also by domestication, and other relations to mankind ; and the surface-changes can be transmitted by constant care to the breeds, and become heredities ; always, however, liable to relapse into the original form,—the *degré brût*, from which they began ; with the instinct still intact, and capable of being developed and varied again and again as at first. But man has no permanent instincts, except in a figurative sense ; and originating from the Creator with a blank mind having freewill and initial conscience within it and above it, and consequently with a capacity for spiritual good, or evil ; for rising or falling in his life ; he is instructible by parents from without and by heaven from within ; and by passive faculties or senses, by reasons, and their upper faculty, intelligence, he can acquire

knowledge, and transmute it into habits not
the result of instincts ; but of the action of a
superior mind or conscience upon an inferior,
or *proprium.* Therefore the more he goes
down in the scale, the less his knowledge or
science is to him; the less considerate his
cerebrum and cerebellum become; the less
of truly human form he transmits to his
offspring; and in the end the inheritance of
the race in him is spent and wasted; and
the hopeless savage appears. The contrary creed, though built through laborious
volumes, seems to us a *magical persuasion*
of the antitheistic mind, in no way differing
in baselessness and irrationality from the
grossest dogmas of theological creeds. It
leaves Man out, not philosophizes towards
him.

The missing Link, and the Link that is not missing.

120. In closing with our friend, the Savage Man, we must notice the "missing link;" for such a gap there is, though in a sense opposite to the scientist view. The chain of creation verily is broken; and, depending, as it does, for its strength upon the will of mankind, it is snapped in the individual and the collective man every day; and in the great Churches which have existed in the world, it is utterly broken for them at the close of the epoch of each. It is the chain that conjoins Man to God; and holds the only Missing Link. "Thou shalt love the Lord thy God above all things, and thy neighbour as thyself. On these two commandments *hang all the Law and the Prophets.*" Here Christ declares the Word

and obedience to its First and Second great commandments, to be a chain; and the actual links of it are the two loves of God and the neighbour perpetually practised in the church of daily life.

121. The link which is not missing is the link which likens, not conjoins, man to the beasts. Descend as he may, he can never be a beast; for no beast can ever do wrong in the sense of disobedience to God's Com - mandments. A tiger is cruel, but not in the sense, or with the delight, that a man is: it is a cruel machine by nature and nature's pleasure, but cannot be a devil. A horse, or a dog, can violate his training, and disappoint his master; but no sane man blames him as a morally, still less as a spiritually, responsible creature. He can succumb to temptation; but he has only one plane, the senses, in which his instincts and reasons lie; and no higher mind to fortify him, or to

rebuke him. He bears immediate, but not remote, consequences. A man, however, can descend below the beasts, and it vilifies them when he is called a beast.

122. Looking thus from above downwards at these two links, the lower and contrarious chain with as many links as there are human evils and lusts, can in no proper scientific sense be said to be missing. As Bacon observes of something else, "it is not deficient but redundant." By its cunning iron hooks it likens and assimilates mankind to the fierce and treacherous creatures of the forest and the wilderness; to serpent and monkey, to wolf and bear, to vulture and crocodile. And yet notwithstanding the broad strands of cerebrum and cerebellum, of flesh and bone, and their delights, which liken him thus to the conscienceless animals, he is blind enough to put on a thousand scientist spectacles to pore after the "missing

link." He does not see the wood for the trees.

123. This all too common link, however,— missed but nowise missing,—is in no affinity with the fabulous monster supposed to be intermediate between man and the beasts. Intermediacy between the possible image of God and possible personification of Satan, and any living machine or zoömagnet, is absurd. The very likeness between the two is in this world a mere analogy. The stream of things from the mineral to man, is a highway of ascending order standing as a pedestal for the human summit; but there is nothing creative in it excepting the Creator; and each part of the series is an end in itself, and terminates a step of the order for itself: its USE making it substantial, and causing its arrest into some fixed form of individuality; or what is the same thing, of service. If it exhausted

itself in the ascent, and became something else, creation would be a bog, and no foundation for the temple it is to bear. But to realize this truth, it is indispensable to be aware by acknowledgment of a creation and also of a Creator. He can realize it for you. But if you make the world out of your own head, or make the world make itself out of its own tail, the savage man in you will engender with the "missing link" also in you, and your faculties will be re-born as mothers of chimæras.

The Africans.

124. By the Savage Man in the preceding pages we understand primarily him whose remains are found in connexion with flint implements and other rude resources of existence; and more inferentially those tribes which are dying out, being unable to enter

either upon property on the earth, or into labour for property as a means of livelihood. This is necessary to be stated; because otherwise some readers might include among such savages ancient nations still extant and abiding; some of whose ways are savage enough, and whose superstitions are manifold and degrading. It may be a problem at any time whether certain races are not dying out; but this speculation we do not touch; but are concerned only with the actual fact of disappearance as the past mark and clear process of the Savage Man.

125. Among the nations which might be taken for granted as savages we will specify the peoples of Africa, and the Negroes in particular. The latter, however, lack the first characteristic of the Savage Man; they do not die out, but are rooted and enduring. They are capable of home life in Africa, and cultivate the soil. Where they have

no contact with the civilized man they are
predatory and brutal; waging incessant wars
with neighbouring tribes; and probably from
old times have been authors and accomplices
in the sale of men, women and children,—in
the initiament of black negro slavery. Yet
as races they are preserved, while so many
of the historical nations, also addicted to the
practice of enslavement, have died out. No
doubt there are reasons for this permanence,
as there are reasons for the perpetuation of
the Jews, the individual nomads of civilization.
We mean deep or spiritual reasons.

126. One great fact is patent about the
captured Negro and also his descendants;
he is of use to the world he lives in. In the
West Indies and in the United States he
demonstrates that he holds his own on this
practical ground. He is a group of industrial
peoples. Evidently what is essential to him
is to have another race over him to enjoin

the duties and morals of his newer existence : where this fails, as in Hayti, he relapses into African conditions. The Frenchman once dispossessed in the island of St. Domingo left him masterful and in ruins. He is probably incapable of any but compulsory civilization. We do not here mean slavery; but the laws and pressures which constitute the existing control of the world ; and which represent our present derivation of the Ten Commandments as influencing Society. The laws of states may be dim reflexions of these, but they are what all honest men have to obey. The Negro has them engrafted upon him, and he is a sufficiently fixed quantity to be capable of enduring the graft, and surviving it. In this sense where there are white men to reign, there are nations of Christian Negroes ; fruitful of progeny, prospering, and promising.

127. Moreover, as we hear, the Negro,

since his emancipation from personal slavery,
is still a labourer for his master, as well as
on his own account ; and raises crops for the
commerce of the world.

128. He has characteristics of his own
apart from those of his white brethren.   As
in all new conditions, he is overweening, and
has not yet found his level as a freedman.
But there lies in him a simple-mindedness
and a religious humility which white Christen-
dom does not possess.   Clever and quick-
seeing, he is incapable of intellectual perversions ; they are nothings to him : dogmas
do not possess him : indeed he has little
of intellect that is separable from his warm
affections.   The very qualities that make
him subservient and utile to the Mahometan,
the Arab and the Turk, are spiritually of
value.   Docility, and not servility but
possible faithful servanthood, stand forth
in him.   The Negroes exemplify service,

and all they want, in order to burn and to
shine, is good masters, or a law-abiding
society around them. They are eminently
capable of affectional religion, and John
Wesley, the man of "dear Jesus," is their
present help in time of need. Labour in
tropic heat, and social skill in common
ministrations, are their quality; and offices
of the affections; for childhood and nursing
are native in the hearts of their women.

129. First of men on this earth, with no
mundane experience about the Negro Race,
Swedenborg, from higher experience, declared
remarkable things about the then hunted and
enslaved blacks, saying that they had in
them a "celestial" genius, and that the good
among them are at last particularly white
in the veracious upper world which shows
us all in our true colours. This is doubtless
the reason that their angels have touched to
the quick the conscience of the nineteenth

century, and that generous-hearted men, the Clarksons, Wilberforces, Lincolns, Emersons, and an army of other good men and women, had no rest day or night until the chains of their slaves were broken. The wars of emancipation have already been mighty for them, and must continue until their homes are safe everywhere under the final olive trees on this earth.

130. Therefore for reasons of nature, use and service; of progeny as the sand of the sea; of affection and religion; yea now of spiritual revelation; and of the manifest help and protection of heaven through human instrumentality; we conclude that the black men are out of the class of the savage man. Their cruel transplantation, which has not destroyed their affections, has made them into orderly and peculiar families of nations; and perhaps in time under white guidance will convert a force of them into armies, for the " redemption,

regeneration, and disenthralment" of their brother-nations in the dark Continent.

PROFESSORS, AND NOT SAVAGES, GUILTY OF MAKING NATURE-MYTHS.

131. As we are here engaged to some extent with the mode of interpretation of mythology, so far as to show that its inner contents demonstrate its origin to be from above, and not from below, we will briefly notice the application of it to nature, which has been attempted by Finn Magnusson for the Scandinavian Mythology, and by other authors and thinkers for the systems of Greece and India, and for other mythologies and myths. See Baring Gould's popular works, *passim.* According to this view, Apollo and the other Gods are nothing else than personifications of the great phenomena of nature. The exploits and fortunes of

Apollo are the changes of the Sun through the Seasons. The Python he slays is the night or the winter; etc. These puerilities are interpretations of the myths from nature to nature; and are of the same kind as the identification of the Great Beast in the Apocalypse with Napoleon Buonaparte, etc. What we have discerned in the myths, is, the remains of a correspondence between *spiritual and not natural* things and the fictitious historicals in the myths. The nature theory, however, would import that the races of men had it in them to anthropomorphize the great and small things of nature, and to set them acting and talking as men and women. But this belongs to the exploded view of the savage man, godless, as the progenitor of the human family; the constitutional seed of language and the arts. No motive can be imagined in him, the prosiest of the prose of outworn human character; for going so far towards poetry, as to make the plain useful sun into a beautiful God ; or to raise external nature, in which the savage was a gravitating element, dying out, into a theatre of supernatural beings, with manifold dramas for its properties. Now evidently the dramatization of nature in mythology, anthropomorphic for the most part as it needs must be, is readily accounted for on the true principle of the fall of man, and is not accounted for on the notion of a self-effected struggle upwards, which is not the known history or lesson of any race. There are many tumbles for nations as for men; but no uprising of the degraded except from without the nature which is in fall. The truth, the Christ in some form, must come to them from without to lift them up : obedience to it in life so lifts them ; and all else is their

N

own gravitation, swifter and more swift, to their end in the dust.

Correspondence is not Analogy. Nature corresponds generally to the Spiritual World, but nothing in Nature to Nature.

132. Nevertheless all nature does correspond to spiritual things, but indirectly. That is to say, not by immediacy of states of life, but through all successions of space and time. Thus the divine Apollo, if we may for a moment clothe Christianity in mythological garments, has the natural Sun with its heat and light corresponding to Him; and it works through nature with His Love and wisdom by its correspondences and material equations. To discern some of these is the highest science, and is a spiritual Philosophy; and they are visible

even in the obscurity of mythology. But mythology itself, already imbedded in nature, leads to nothing but arbitrary fancy work when it is carried out as meaning nature, and not mind and spirit. It is the old story of materialism, now so prevalent in many fields. You have your Man given, your Apollo, and instead of conversing with his interior life through his plain face, and understanding him, you vivisect him into Nature's Sun and Moon, and in the end convert him into dust and ashes. The Greeks did indeed turn correspondences into fabulous matter; but they were still correspondences though perverted, corrupted, and debased; and they were never the almanacs or weather-registers of the savage man.

133. The fixed field of nature, with the iron-clanking rule of space and time directing it, is no platform to which even myth and

mythology can apply themselves. They are borrowed from man's spirit, and are significant there only. Sunrise and sunset, thunder and lightning, are sunrise, sunset, thunder and lightning, and cannot be recast into other forms. But on the spiritual side these natural words in the Word all dwell *in* man, are therefore anthropomorphic for good or evil; and in declining races this character comes manifestly forth in a crowd of Gods and goddesses, and natural super-natures and superstitions. (Of these Dr. William Smith reckons that there were some thirty thousand in the Greek mythology alone.)

Human Nature is all compact of Consan-guinities, Ancestries and Heredities, genuine Families of Mental States.

134. There is a law in human nature as it goes onwards to its manifold goals and be-

gettings, by which all things have progeny, and are as fathers, mothers, sons and daughters in the unrolling of time. The advance pushes back the fathers into grand-fathers; and at length into remote ancestors and "most ancient" peoples. The seed is there, and the river which we now are comes from the first head-waters of it. So it is with mythology also. Its Grandsire is revelation of the spiritual world. Its Father is the recorded memory and use of this revelation for another church. Mythology itself is the wandering Ishmael, the child of the bondwoman, or of a spurious but still necessary religion. The interpretation is the last thing, and follows the fates of the fontal revelation. The *finale* always is to sink the entire drama of the once celestial and spiritual man into nature and modern language, and to consume its ashes there. This is the scientist and philosophast road

towards the savage man. It occurred in
Asia and in Egypt, and probably presided
at the nomenclature of the constellations.
If there were not still a revealed Lord God,
the end of it would be universal metaphysics,
and then, failing nourishment on their east
wind, mental suicide of disgust and despair.

Comparative Mythology : its new
Christian Value.

135. Comparative mythology is not charge-
able with this, but should be versed in tracing
the likeness and parallelism of Myths in
various races and ages ; and also in purging
the true mythological body from the accretions
of fancy and imagination, which are not the
factors of genuine myths. For instance, when
the cows of Audhumbla [1] are said to be the ice-

---

[1] The derivation of these words is marked as uncertain in the
Lexicons ; but *Saehrimnir* seems likest to the rime or foam of the

bergs, it is clear that fancy frames the cypher and the analogue. Also when the boar Saehrimnir, the ever-renewed banquet of the Æsir in Valhalla, is alive and whole every morning after being eaten in the midday repast, and is named from the foam of the sea, which foam never suffers, or fails, we plainly see that poetry is at work; and that it has caught hold of a huge analogy of unfailing supply. It is a simile used as a correspondence. The boar-coinage gives a rude richness to the table. But here the whole platform is from nature to nature; and though there is a mental element and suggestion in the conceit, it has no spiritual contents, and mythology washes its hands

sea; and if Audhumbla is from Audhr = void, and húm = darkness, it may mean the polar darkness, of which the icebergs are the fed and feeding cows. This is not myth, but the common allegorizing habit of the poetical Norse language. See Sveinbjörn Egillson's *Lexicon Poeticum* throughout. The rime of the sea is a storm-food, and is appropriate to the fighting dynasty which reigned in Valhalla. If they had a second course it might be Mother Carey's chickens.

of it. When the study of "comparative mythology" is advanced, it forms a valuable attestation of the great network of heathenism as having a universality and organic oneness which proclaims its descent from the earliest and the early religions and Churches of Jehovah. An opinion indeed prevails that the multitudinous myths which resemble Bible things, discredit and disprove the sacred character of the latter; but when once it is established that the Word not only stands above, but in time precedes, all heathenisms; and that the highest humanity was at the beginning, and because it was at the beginning will again be at the end; this other opinion, dear to a school of naturalists, falls to the ground. Now the previous position *is* established in the *Arcana Cœlestia* and the great series of Swedenborg's Writings.

136. Baring Gould well says in his chapter

on the "Legend of the Cross," that it is founded on the fact "that the cross was a sacred sign long before Christ died upon it. And how account for this? . . . I see no difficulty in believing that it formed a portion of the primeval religion, traces of which exist over the whole world among every people. . . . The use of the cross as a symbol of life and regeneration . . . is as widely spread over the world as the belief in the ark of Noah."

CORRESPONDENCES ARE THE ADMINISTRATORS OF DIVINE JUSTICE AND JUDGMENT.

137. Bear now in mind in judging of the foregoing little treatise, that Correspondences as they are here meant, are extant *only in the Inspired Word;* and that it is the perversion of *these* correspondences which gave rise to all the mythologies. For the Word is

written in natural language, but according to the laws and visible appearances *of the spiritual world.* This constitutes it the medium of communication between the Lord and the Church, between heaven and earth. And the spiritual world is quite similar in outward appearance to the natural world, and contains in its immensity all the objects of universal nature, and indefinitely more besides. But it differs from the lower or natural creation in this one respect, that each thing, realm and sphere of it corresponds by divine justice and mercy to the individuals, societies, and greater and greatest organizations, of the angels and spirits, of the human people, who are in it. Hence in designating any object; as sun, moon, and stars; as domestic or wild animals; as birds or fishes; as trees or plants; as stones or minerals; the spiritual quality of the individual and the society of which the apparent object is

the outcome, is the matter intended in the
Word. You might read the *quale* of the
society in the turf it treads on and in the
trees which embosom it. The objects in
fact are the mere appearances of human
states of good and evil, truth and falsity;
they are virtues and vices embodied. Such
being the case, they represent and signify
with infinite variety all those things in man;
and because they represent and signify, they
correspond to them. In this ultimate, fixed
and lower world *nothing so represents, signifies, or corresponds.* The sun shines upon
the evil and the good; the summer warms
and the winter chills them both alike. But
there is no winter in heaven; because the
hearts there are devoid of the love of self,
which is spiritual cold; and there is no sun
in hell; because the infinite Love shuts
itself away by merciful impassable barriers
from those whose evil freedom it would

infringe; and whom therefore its ardent fire
of unselfishness would destroy.   These then
are specimens of the correspondences which
were universally contained and perceived by
the men of the first Church and most ancient
Religion.   They were intuitively known by
the transfluence of heaven where such correspondences are the law, through their minds
open to angelic influence and conversation.
The Word in them was a constant and in-
tuitive communication, written on their souls,
and flowing through their perceptions into
their senses.   And hence the objects of this
world seemed also to be correspondential by
constantly suggesting their spiritual similars
in the celestial abodes.   This was in the
beginning of God's Fatherhood, and of the
religion of His infantine children kneeling
around Him; and this is what in its extinction died out into the several planes of
mythology.

Help from Swedenborg.

138. To enable the reader to comprehend more easily the perceptive state of the earliest men, by some analogy with the condition of the human mind to-day, and to show that there is no realism of things which outlies the characteristic states of the will, or which, as Bacon phrases it, is not " steeped in the affections," we cite the following passage from Swedenborg.

139. " For the men of the most ancient Church there was no other than internal worship ; such worship as exists in heaven, for heaven so communicated with man in them, that the two made one. This communication consisted in the PERCEPTION often spoken of above. Therefore because the internal man in them was angelic, they were sensible indeed of the external things

belonging to the body and the world, but
they did not care for them.   In all the
objects of the senses they perceived a something divine and celestial.   For example,
when they saw a high mountain, they did
not perceive the idea of the mountain, but
the idea of height; and in the height they saw
heaven, and the Lord.   Hence it came to
pass that the Lord was said to dwell in the
highest, and Himself was called the most
High and the most Ex-cellent; and afterwards the worship of the Lord was held on
mountains.   So again when they perceived
the morning, it was not the mere morning
of the day, but the celestial morning, the
morning and dawn in the mind.   Hence
the Lord was the Morning, the East and
the Dawn.   So when they saw a tree with
its fruit and leaves, they did not heed these
at all, but they saw man in them ; love and
charity in the fruit; and faith in the leaves.

Hence the man of the Church was not only compared to a tree, and to a Paradise, and his endowments to fruit and leaves, but he was also called these very names. Such are those who live in the celestial and angelic idea. Men of every capacity can understand that each general or common idea rules all the particulars which belong to it; for instance, all the objects of the senses, all which the mind of the man sees, or hears; and in such wise rules them, that he takes no heed to the objects save in so far as they enter into his general idea. To him who is glad at heart, all the things which he hears and sees appear joyous and smiling. But to the sorrowful man all are sad and distressing. So it is in every case. The general affection is in all its circumstances, and makes the man see and hear whatever is about him in that affection. The rest is irrelevant and non-apparent, absent and nothing to him. Apply

this to the man of the Most Ancient Church.
Whatever he saw with his eyes was for him
celestial ; and all and singular things were in
a manner alive.   From this the nature of his
Divine Worship may be clearly seen.   It
was internal and in no wise external.   But
the Church declined in his posterity, and
then the above-mentioned perception, the
communication with heaven, began to perish,
and a different order of things arose.   Men
then no longer perceived the Celestial in the
objects of the senses as heretofore, but the
mundane, and this, more and more as the
residue of perception grew smaller.   And
in the last posterity immediately before the
flood they found nothing in objects but
worldly, bodily, and earthly things.   So
heaven was separated from man, and
only communicated with him very remotely.
Communication with hell was then brought
to pass; and the general idea, the origin

of the ideas of all the particulars, came from thence. Then when any celestial idea offered itself, it was a thing of naught, and at last man refused to acknowledge the existence of the spiritual and celestial at all. In fact the state was changed and turned upside down. As this event was foreseen by the Lord, provision was made, that the doctrinals of faith should be conserved, so that mankind might know from them what the celestial was, and what the spiritual. Those who were called Cain and Enoch collected these doctrinals from the Man of the Most Ancient Church : and therefore it is said of Cain that a mark was put upon him, that no one might slay him ; and of Enoch, that he was taken by God. These doctrinals consisted merely in significatives, and in a manner in enigmatic cyphers ; they declared what the things upon earth signified ; to wit, the mountains ; namely things in heaven,

and the Lord. What the morning and the
East; namely again things in heaven, and
the Lord. What the different kinds of trees
and their fruits signified ; man namely, and
the celestial things belonging to him. Their
doctrinals consisted of such teachings collected
from the significatives of the Most Ancient
Church. Their writings therefore were of
the same character. And as they admired
and seemed to themselves to behold a divine
and celestial character in such things, and
also because of their antiquity, so worship
had inception, and was permitted, out of
these and the like teachings ; and was
held on mountains, in groves, and among
trees. Hence too their pillars in the
open air : and ultimately their altars and
burnt offerings ; which became in the end
the principal forms in all worship. This
worship originating from the Ancient Church,
spread to its posterity, and to all the

nations round about." (*Arcana Cœlestia*, n. 920.)

140. This extract translated somewhat freely, gives a synopsis from one point of the Most Ancient Man, and of the Ancient Man; and restates all we have had to say on Revelation and Mythology. It is fruitful in many directions. It leads to consider what the life of the most internal men was, seeing that they also had daily duties in the natural world, and did them from instantaneous perception. The Paradise which they inhabited, truly adult in love and its wisdom as they were, was a fostering cradle to the celestial good that was in them. They were not students or philosophers, but veritable working seers engaged with the truest life in close company with angels; and the central beatitude of nature was in a sense both their church and their mother. They were not therefore lost in their own perceptions, as

the superficial reader might imagine, but
they saw things as they really were; full of
God, and binding to love, light, and conduct
in every dear human relation.   Nor was appreciation lost but heightened and intensified
by seeing things through and through as
optic words of twelvefold crystal; but each
stair of perception was a sublime resting-
place for thankfulness and delight.   Art may
picture this, and the Poet imagine towards
it, but it is a lost divine art to live it.   We
forbear to venture further on an endless
theme.   This state, therefore, so remote
from man and nature to-day, is not a dream
of idlesse, but a supreme theatre of use and
service.

141. See on this subject Bishop South's
fine sermon on the state of Adam.   I read it
long years ago.   For lack of knowledge now
given, the Bishop regarded Adam as a single
person, and not as the primeval or Most

Ancient Church; and was not aware that
the *Flood-ages* intervened destructively between that Church and subsequent mankind.
He says however truly that the mind of
Adam lived " in direct fervours of love to
God, and in collateral emissions of charity
to Man." I quote from memory. Also that
" an Aristotle was but the ruins of an Adam."
We may say that glacial epochs of heathenism,
in which providential effacement of whole
planes of human life and its kingdoms
occurred, intervened between the Greek
mind and the Ancient Church. Aristotle
was not therefore a ruin in any relation to
Adam; but a new and lower point of departure, with service in his great faculty
for many generations, to the present time;
perhaps contributing some organic sinews
to the doctrinal body of truths which are
now revealed to us.

142. Finally in treating of the inward life

of the first men, that is, of the most ancient Church, we find their derivatives in the correspondences collected and preserved by Cain and Enoch, and serving as Media for the two succeeding Churches down to the coming of Christ; when the outward use of Correspondences, excepting in the case of Baptism and the Holy Supper, ceased. But of the most Ancient Church itself there are no other direct remains : as the first divine making of a *collective* man it is extinct. It was changed into a new condition of religion in the secondary humanity called Noah ;—in the Noahtic Church. Nevertheless it is not extinct as a life; but reappears personally and individually wherever man or woman by regeneration is opened into the celestial degree of affection and perception. Such scattered instances are the seed and promise of the second golden ages of the New Jerusalem ; which city will comprise all sorts and conditions of men, natural, spiritual, and celestial. But with regard to the Most Ancient Church as an inspired organ raising up the human family to become the immediate sons of Jehovah God, the only possible record of it is by the correspondences in the Sacred Scripture. This is intimately internal-historical, and not external ; it stands within and above History, and is the beginning of the present Word ; related indeed to all subsequent records, and illuminating them : but the frailty and transiency of the celestial state, as it were morning dew, and of its successions, demands, what it has, nothing less than a divine recorder.

The Origin of Language.

143. Among the things involved in the creation of man is also the origin of language. For the Man here meant, coming by virtue

of Creation direct from Jehovah God, is the
Celestial Man, often spoken of above. He
carried in him and with him the first fortunes
of the human race, and was a man of all
heavenly gifts in the conditions of nature.
He perceived that all he was and had was
free gift, and also that in this perception
alone he was able to take it and to keep it.

144. One of these divine gifts was language
as an expressive organ of human love and
its wisdom. It was given for intercourse
with God in worship, in praise and thanks-
giving; and in prayer. Also for intercourse
with angels. And for the association on all
grounds of man with man ; for it begot the
introduction of man to his fellows ; it welded
him into a society. Like his brain, his heart
and his lungs, it was an organic inspiration
in him, for, living soul and living body, he
was himself a momentaneous inspiration :
with a finite freewill and a percipient mind

to receive it. (Genesis ii. 7 ; Luke iii. 38.) His speech was a language of correspondences ; he called natural things by celestial names. It was adequate and answerable to the whole ground of things; for this is implied in correspondence. When he named the creatures from their perceived or self-evident celestial origin, Jehovah assented ; the speech through him was a creation like the creatures themselves : it was as it were the Word written on his heart, warm and luminous, speaking.

145. This language was both visible and audible in the beginning ; it was both volume and speech. The celestial face of Man was the volume. The eyes and the lips, and the entire open sanctuary of expression, corresponded organically to the innocence, wisdom and sincerity within. The face, nowise double, was the most consummate and definite language, a varying

tablet of the constant effluxes of the soul : a human Shekinah of words of light.

146. The voice was lower and secondary in place and perfection. It also corresponded, but more outwardly, to the same intimate affections and perceptions of the man : it was inspirationally automatic as well as freely voluntary.

147. All this follows, as we now know by revelation, from the concept of the Celestial Man ; and his Creation by Jehovah. For the Celestial man, the Most Ancient Church, is the key to religious history ; and ultimately to mundane History. It is the Church of the primeval gifts and origins, and the substance of their survivals.

148. It also follows from the same ground that the human form and organism was at the beginning in the Adam a natural celestial form ; capable of loving and receiving such supreme gifts, and finding blessedness in them.

They were given because they could not be
otherwise acquired. They are revealed now,
revealed rationally, because to discover them
otherwise is beyond the reach of the human
understanding. By contrast therefore we
now perceive that the human form as we
possess it, is not what it was when it
came fresh from the hands of its Creator and
Maker. It is not now His image, or likeness,
except internally by regeneration, the outward signature of which awaits its manifestation in the spiritual world. At present, a
thousand ages have deposited the seeds
of actual sin, and the evils of inheritance,
within it, and deformed its primeval state.
Eye and lip and voice have carried out
these degradations, and the seats of life
are truncated, disfibrated and confused.
The lapsing man becomes withered and
extinct, not abstractly but organically, and
the regenerate man must be born again

organically. The human form of the Adamic "likeness" of Jehovah God cannot therefore be submitted in thought even anatomically to any argument or criterion derived from the bodies and powers of men at the present day.

149. The words of the first or Most Ancient Man, full of direct perception, had no thought in them as we use and reckon thought. They were Yea, Yea, and Nay, Nay, each with a whole significance; cumbrous with no hieroglyphics, and subtle with no obscurities. They were not spoken from, or modified by, anything we call intellect; but were merely sonorous with love, and vocal with wisdom.

150. Language thus given to mankind as a constitutional endowment, it was with it as with the Science of Correspondences; it was perpetuated in declining ages by the ear and the memory; that is to say, so much of it was

traditive as did not evanesce and perish in its delivery to the lower human nature after the Flood; since which event it has come down in its many streams to this day. See Swedenborg, *Arcana Cœlestia*, vol. i., chaps. i-xi. Also like the most ancient Correspondences, of which it was an expressive part, it has given rise to its own Mythologies. These are the attempts of earth-born Science to invent an origin for, and an account of, the divine gift of speech : which are the verbose myths of the learned.

151. We are therefore again warned to desist from seeking the origin of language from the eloquence of the appetites of a prehistoric life, which has no existence but in the speechless beasts. The beasts however have their pregnant lesson; they come provided with sufficient tongues, as Man came; they have the two endowments, of expressive features and sounds, given in their bodies and natures,

of adequate use and meaning for their loves and lives.

152. We conclude that a natal celestial Word written on man's heart was the beginning of human speech; that a revelation has made this known; and that the Creator's Omnipotent Word itself is the origin of language.

REVELATION AND MYTHOLOGY.

153. The ground of Revelation is that the Lord God created mankind from the dust of the lowest natural state, through Freewill which is individual man, into His Image and Likeness.   The spiritual man—intelligence —is His image, and the celestial man— Love—is His likeness.   Revelation and the Creation of Man or Adam are coequal and coeval, indeed identical.   God, turning His face to His creature, is a divine and

infinite Man. All thought which truly and lovingly knows Him, sees His human divinity and divine humanity. What is the same thing, He is Our Father. He spoke to Man in His own speech made man's speech, as from the first his creator, instructor, and Redeemer. The Word is His speech. First it was written in Man's heart, inspired as perception there, and breathed forth by man in ineffable thoughts and namings, the heavens of language. The entire Adam spoke it. The divine-human form reigned by love; a form inalienable and incorruptible. It holds man by bonds that cannot be broken. Man strove with it and inverted his own humanity. But the form was with him still: it involves the root principle of the world and of every creature. So in Mythology there is nothing but the human form, or derivatives of it. Through fetish, through idols of wood and

stone, whether vegetable, serpentine, animal,
or human, this necessity, human form, survived, as the ground and spring of embodiment.   All can be assigned back to the
Word and its Correspondences.   This is
the conclusion shorn of details.   God and
religion are personal, and mythology is
derivatively personal.   Infinite man and
finite man are the agents.   At peace together, or not at peace.   Historically and
theologically the gap of ages is bridged over,
and become a highway in the divine Genesis
since the veil of the letter is lifted up.

APPENDIX.

——o——

EXPLANATORY OF TERMS.

154. A few words are used in the foregoing pages in a sense requiring explanation. The word *Celestial* throughout as applied to Man or Adam signifies the inspired man of the affections with their perceptions: the affections of love to God and the neighbour; and the perceptions of wisdom that enable the man to carry such affections into Works. The word *Spiritual* belongs to the man of conscience and its intelligence, acted on from without by the divine truths of the commandments; the supremacy of duty to God and man being the spiritual man's life. On this subject Swedenborg says: "There are two loves according to which the heavens are

P

distinguished, celestial love, and spiritual love : celestial love is love to the Lord, and spiritual love is love towards the neighbour. These loves are distinguished by this, that celestial love is the love of good, and spiritual love is the love of truth ; for those who are in celestial love do uses from the love of good, and those who are in spiritual love do uses from the love of truth. The marriage of celestial love is with wisdom, and the marriage of spiritual love is with intelligence ; for it is wisdom's way to do good from good, but it is the way of intelligence to do good from truth : wherefore celestial love doeth good, and spiritual love doeth truth." The word *Proprium* has been sometimes employed, because there is no complete English term for it. *Amour propre*, in a fundamental sense, may be correlative to it in French. The proper selfhood or individual nature of the man is implied ; the ruling natural love embedded in the sensual plane or degree, full of the evils of the character, hereditary and actual. Its organic function is to react against the faculties and motives above it. And being outermost, it holds and binds every man to his own personality. The more he has of it under subjection, the higher he can become by regeneration. The *Proprium* is the battlefield of Heaven and Hell in man.

EGYPT, ASSYRIA, ISRAEL.

155. Egypt, where it is mentioned in the Word, always signifies the natural man, specifically with regard to his mind in its capacity and desire for knowledges (cognitions) and sciences on their own account, or to gratify and carry out the *proprium*. Assyria always signifies the rational man, the ratiocinator or rationalist. Israel is the spiritual man, over

whom divine truth is in power. These
significations belong indeed to the Ancient
Church, but apply to mankind for ever. The
text on the title-page is therefore clear. It
is a prophecy of the order when what is
spiritual reigns by free choice in the mind's
several parts of influence and power. First,
a new state signified by "that day;" and
then a highway for informations and experiences from the active collecting and
knowing mind into the active reason above
it: a highway from Egypt to Assyria.
Then as an end for the way so far, commerce
of consociation, between science and right
reason; the entry of science into the rational
man, and of the rational man into the
scientific: each limiting and enlarging the
other to its own conditions: the Egyptian
first coming to Ashur; and then the
Assyrian into Egypt: experience gathered
from without, the basis of thought: reason,

so far, the provisional judge. Up to this
point the history of the opening natural mind
is written down in these correspondences of
nations. As a condition of this highway of
commerce between them, the Egyptian is to
serve with the Assyrian; those two great
abodes of the *amour propre*, science and the
reasoning power, are both to acknowledge
that they are servants, and that they are
willing to own to a mind from above. They
need its control to be of human use. Another
new state is now proclaimed in the words
repeated, "that day." It is the voice of the
mind's Master, the spiritual man. He comes
unobtrusively: Israel is to be the third with
Egypt and Assyria; the third is the com-
pletion, the three in one, the all in all. Such
is the signification of three in its fractions
and in the whole. The freewill ruling now
resides in the Israel, and is its especial faculty,
and science and reason belong to revealed

Truth : a blessing in the midst of the land.
The midst is the inmost; the land is the
Lord's Church : Egypt and Assyria are both
within it; free and fruitful : and the blessing
of serving the spiritual faculties of man is
their portion and wealth.   Observe the place
of Egypt as first in time in the threefold
unity.   The knowledges, of Correspondences
and the like, are implied; and a new spiritual
and natural life.

156. We see from this statement that
humanity is created in spiritual and psychical
planes, in diversities of genius and genus,
corresponding to national characteristics and
geographical sites and climates.   And being
one body, a mundane representative of the
Maximus Homo above, each of these national
minds, Egypt, Assyria, Israel and others, is
a different part of the universal man.   In
modern times also, as Swedenborg says,
there are nations corresponding in their

places to the Biblical Nations of the old world. So this earth and the dwellers in it are nothing less than a veiled mind of the most specialized organic description : if you will, a cerebrum and cerebellum with all their world of dependent nerves. The collective genius of each race is however spiritually unknown in the world excepting where the Word has revealed it. The history of each, its wars and destinies, is the outcome of its character as a province in the great human form.

Bacon's View of Mythology.

157. A few extracts from Bacon's *Wisdom of the Ancients* will show how the mind of the reputed modern Father of Induction reached forward towards a later and greater light.

158. " The earliest antiquity," Bacon says,

" lies buried in silence and oblivion, excepting
the remains we have of it in Sacred Writ.
This silence was succeeded by poetical fables ;
and these, at length, by the writings we
now enjoy : so that the concealed and secret
learning of the ancients seems separated from
the history and knowledge of the following
ages, by a veil, or partition-wall of fables,
interposing between the things that are lost,
and the things that remain."

159. " It would be rash and almost profane, to detract from the honour of allegory
and parable in general.   For since religion
delights in such shadows and disguises, to
abolish these were, in a manner, to prohibit
all intercourse betwixt things divine and
human."

160. Here is a foregleam of the function of
Correspondences in the Word, as understood
on their respective planes in both worlds,
and thus as constituting a divine means of

union between the two,—between heaven and earth.

161. Again—" Many of these fables by no means appear to have been invented by the persons who relate and divulge them ; whether Homer, Hesiod, or others. Whoever attentively considers the thing, will find that they are delivered down by those writers, not as matters then first invented and proposed, but as things received and embraced in earlier ages. As they are differently related by writers nearly contemporaneous, it is easily perceived that the relaters drew from a common stock of ancient tradition. This principally raises my esteem of these fables ; which I receive, not as the product of the age, or invention of the Poets, but as sacred relics, gentle whispers, and the breath of better times ; which from the traditions of more ancient nations, came at length

into the flutes and trumpets of the Greeks."

162. " In the first ages . . . all things abounded with fables, parables, similes, comparisons, and allusions; which were not intended to conceal, but to inform, and teach. . . . As hieroglyphics were in use before writing, so were parables in use before arguments. And even to this day, if any man would let new light in upon the human understanding, and conquer prejudice, without raising contests, animosities, oppositions, or disturbance, he must still go in the same path, and have recourse to the like method of allegory, metaphor and allusion. The *knowledge* of the early ages was either great, or happy; great, if they by design made this use of trope and figure; happy, if whilst they had other views, their knowledge afforded matter and occasion to noble contemplations."

163. " The ancient Mythology seems to us like a vintage ill pressed and trod; for though something has been drawn from it, yet all the more excellent parts remain behind, in the grapes that are untouched."

164. Here is another passage worthy of record :—

" It may pass for a further indication of a concealed and secret meaning, that some of these fables are so absurd, and idle, in their narration, as to show and proclaim an allegory even afar off. A fable that carries probability with it, may be supposed to be invented for pleasure, or in imitation of history; but those fables that could never be conceived, or related in this way, must surely have a different use. For example, what a monstrous fiction is this, that Jupiter should take Metis to wife; and as soon as he found her pregnant, eat her up; whereby he also conceived, and out of his head

brought forth Pallas armed? Certainly
no mortal could, but for the sake of the
moral it couches, invent such an absurd
dream : so much out of the road of
thought."

165. It is no part of the object of these
pages to furnish interpretations of the ancient
myths excepting cursorily and incidentally,
the main purpose being to indicate that they
have not only a most ancient, but the highest
primordial origin and golden record. Bacon
shows here that their very strangeness is a
witness to their eminent capacity of contents.
It is not indeed every odd metamorphosis
or incongruous story of which this can be
inferred. But when we find a myth occur-
ring in a mythological system many parts of
which openly display an arcane sense; and
that system repeated for several races of
men in collateral forms, we may safely infer
that such a myth cannot be set aside as a

magazine of absurdity. Many parts of mythology are indeed isolated inventions, about which we may use a phrase of Montaigne, that "their inanity gives them reverence and weight;" they being unduly received among the noble myths, and so coming within the scope of popular credulity. Even this however is a proof of mythic power and influence derived from the body of true mythology. But for the other sort, their perturbation of parts and movements, their unnaturalness in short, only shows that they are deflected from all common form by a planet of meanings above them and within them. That is *their* Mathesis.

166. Bacon as a Natural Philosopher of History, and man of the State, assigned to many of the Myths a political signification, particularly with regard to public order ; the means and managements for conserving it; and the rights, duties and counsels of kings :

also, the Typhons, swellings, and insurrections that threaten States or Establishments; and what the ends of disturbers are, and how they themselves end. In this he in nowise strained the rights of the method he took deliberately in hand, as the way of founding the knowledge of nature including human nature on a new basis of certainty. For if mythological narrations as quasi-historic can be opened upwards into spiritual series, as he often attempted, and can correspond to the truths of the soul as Revelation imparts them, so they can be opened at the side upon the theatre of general social disposition and action, which is an ultimate outcome of the spiritual states of the Collective man. Here we have a justification of the manifold meanings brought out of Holy Scripture, and also out of the Myths which are descended from it in heathen nations. These correspondential cyphers are for all time,

and turn a diurnal face to human life and all
that it is on all its planes and tiers, ascending
and descending. The mind objects that
the Vala or Prophetess, of the Myth for
instance, never thought of to-day's interpretation, still less intended it. Not consciously indeed, but generatively; for the
Myth-form is not artistic or philosophical,
but pre-eminently and actively generative.
Its faculty and business of generation knows
not that any children will proceed from it,
nor what children, nor what the first
child contains. Sufficient that it is legitimate, and owned by a spiritual father. To
every myth worth the name there is therefore a spiritual sense, a moral sense, and a
political and social sense; and these vary
like light and heat; and like love, duty, and
works; with the days; and are inexhaustible.
The tripod authors of the myths are the
passive mothers of them, and utter no voice

against an interminable progeny.   Only the
sense and application must always be, as
Bacon says, *in majorem Dei Gloriam*, and
also *ad usus humanos;* a condition in which
he is divinely reinforced by Swedenborg.

INDEX.

—o—

Q

THE END.

MORRISON AND GIBB, EDINBURGH,
PRINTERS TO HER MAJESTY'S STATIONERY OFFICE.

www.ingramcontent.com/pod-product-compliance
Lightning Source LLC
Chambersburg PA
CBHW020853270326
41928CB00006B/680